Python Code Warrior-Working with WMI

Working Windows Management Instrumentation and creating reports By Example

Richard Thomas Edwards

This book is dedicated to the technical support people I worked with at Microsoft from 1996 to 2002. We were the best of the best at what we did. Thank you all!

CONTENTS

Why WMI

More than what meets the eye

*When you are totally committed to getting
something done, only death can stop you.*
—*R. T. Edwards*

Once upon a time, I worked for John Wanamaker's store in Moorestown, New
Jersey. A movie was filmed at the John Wanamaker's store in Philadelphia
called *The Mannequin* and the theme song was "Nothing's going to stop us."
It was sung by Jefferson Starship. One day in the summer of 1993, my makeup was
on stage with that group.

Life has its own strange way of weaving fate in a positive way if your mind is set
on making what you truly believe in and is part of your life's work.

Which brings me to why I decided to write this book and why you should find
this book worth your time reading and working with what is here, so you can add
this expertise and, perhaps, find employment using Python with WMI.

With that said, let's begin your WMI journey with defining what WMI is.

WMI is an abbreviation for Windows Management Instrumentation and has been
around for the past 20 years. It was originally called WBEM or Web Based Enterprise
Management.

It is free and if you are running windows, it is already on your machine.

Back in 1998 the number of classes WMI supported was around 4,000. Today,
that number has increased to around 12,000. When you install SQL Server or any
other large program such as Office or Visual Studio, that number can easily double.

WMI has a hierarchy. Meaning, there are namespaces and these point to classes that you can use to find out a lot of interesting information about your machine. When I ran the code below, there was a total of 219 of them.

Namespaces

```
import win32com.client

def EnumNamespaces(nspace):
print nspace
strComputer = "."
l = win32com.client.Dispatch("WbemScripting.SWbemLocator")
svc = l.ConnectServer(strComputer, nspace)
svc.Security_.AuthenticationLevel = 6
svc.Security_.ImpersonationLevel = 3
objs = svc.InstancesOf("___NAMESPACE")
for obj in objs:
EnumNamespaces(nspace + "\\" + obj.Name)


EnumNamespaces("root")
```

But the most popular one both on the internet and with most programmers, is the one below:

```
root\CIMV2
```

Classes

The win32_ classes without the perf counters comes out to 420 and I have – I'm sure you don't either – any interest is a 3-page spread of Win32 Classes which – unless you are planning on using then – take up precious space in this e-book.

However, if you want to see what's on your machine using any namespace and not just root\cimv2, below is the code:

```
import win32com.client
```

```
strComputer = "."
l = win32com.client.Dispatch("WbemScripting.SWbemLocator")
svc = l.ConnectServer(strComputer, "root\\cimv2")
svc.Security_.AuthenticationLevel = 6
svc.Security_.ImpersonationLevel = 3
objs = svc.SubClassesOf()
for obj in objs:
print obj.Path_.Class
```

The ones I like working with are:

Win32_BIOS
Win32_COMClass
Win32_ComputerSystem
Win32_LogicalDisk
Win32_NetworkAdapter
Win32_NetworkLogonProfile
Win32_OperatingSystem
Win32_Process
Win32_Processor
Win32_Product
Win32_Service
Win32_VideoController

Properties

```
import win32com.client
import string

strComputer = "."
l = win32com.client.Dispatch("WbemScripting.SWbemLocator")
svc = l.ConnectServer(strComputer, "root\\cimv2")
svc.Security_.AuthenticationLevel = 6
svc.Security_.ImpersonationLevel = 3
obj = svc.Get("Win32_ComputerSystem")
for prop in obj.Properties_:
print prop.Name
```

And the list from Win32_ComputerSystem is:

AdminPasswordStatus
AutomaticManagedPagefile
AutomaticResetBootOption
AutomaticResetCapability
BootOptionOnLimit
BootOptionOnWatchDog
BootROMSupported
BootStatus
BootupState
Caption
ChassisBootupState
ChassisSKUNumber
CreationClassName
CurrentTimeZone
DaylightInEffect
Description
DNSHostName
Domain
DomainRole
EnableDaylightSavingsTime
FrontPanelResetStatus
HypervisorPresent
InfraredSupported
InitialLoadInfo
InstallDate
KeyboardPasswordStatus
LastLoadInfo
Manufacturer
Model
Name
NameFormat
NetworkServerModeEnabled
NumberOfLogicalProcessors
NumberOfProcessors
OEMLogoBitmap
OEMStringArray

PartOfDomain
PauseAfterReset
PCSystemType
PCSystemTypeEx
PowerManagementCapabilities
PowerManagementSupported
PowerOnPasswordStatus
PowerState
PowerSupplyState
PrimaryOwnerContact
PrimaryOwnerName
ResetCapability
ResetCount
ResetLimit
Roles
Status
SupportContactDescription
SystemFamily
SystemSKUNumber
SystemStartupDelay
SystemStartupOptions
SystemStartupSetting
SystemType
ThermalState
TotalPhysicalMemory
UserName
WakeUpType
Workgroup

Methods

```
import win32com.client
import string

strComputer = "."
l = win32com.client.Dispatch("WbemScripting.SWbemLocator")
svc = l.ConnectServer(strComputer, "root\\cimv2")
svc.Security_.AuthenticationLevel = 6
```

```
svc.Security_.ImpersonationLevel = 3
obj = svc.Get("Win32_ComputerSystem")
for Method in obj.Methods_:
print Method.Name
```

The results:

    SetPowerState
    Rename
    JoinDomainOrWorkgroup
    UnjoinDomainOrWorkgroup

Communicating with WMI
The devil is in the details

Without effort, nothing gets done.
Without knowing defeat, you cannot know true
success.
—R. T. Edwards

N| ow that you've gotten a taste of what some of the namespaces are and what classes one single namespace may expose, let's turn our attention to the mechanics of working with that information.

There are two ways to connect to the WMI resources using Python:

- WbemScripting.SWbemLocator
- Winmgmts

While booth can connect to remote machines, only one has enables you to pass in a UserName and Password and that is WbemScripting.SWbemLocator.

As for winmgmts – Which can be typed Winmgmts or WinMgmts, there is a very good article on the subject which can be found here. Right now, I want to focus on the WbemScripting.SWbemLocator.

Connection Options

Below are some of the ways you will see this used:

Local Connection Options

```
l = win32com.client.Dispatch("WBemScripting.SWbemLocator")

s = l.ConnectServer()
s = l.ConnectServer(".", "root\\cimv2")
s = l.ConnectServer(".", "root\\cimv2", "","", "MS_0409")
s = l.ConnectServer(".", "root\\cimv2", "", "", "MS_0409", "", 128)
s = l.ConnectServer(".", "root\\cimv2", "", "", "MS_0409", "", 128, None)
```

Or:

```
s = l.ConnectServer("Localhost", "root\\cimv2")
s = l.ConnectServer("Localhost", "root\\cimv2", "", "", "MS_0409")
s = l.ConnectServer("Localhost", "root\\cimv2", "", "", "MS_0409", "", 128)
s = l.ConnectServer("Localhost", "root\\cimv2", "", "", "MS_0409","", 128,
None)
```

Remote Connection Options

```
s = l.ConnectServer()
s = l.ConnectServer("RMachine", "root\\cimv2")
s = l.ConnectServer("RMachine", "root\\cimv2", "UserName", "Password",
"MS_0409")
s = l.ConnectServer("RMachine", "root\\cimv2", "UserName", "Password",
"MS_0409", "", 128)
s = l.ConnectServer("RMachine", "root\\cimv2", "UserName", "Password",
"MS_0409", "", 128, None)
```

RMachine, of course being the machine, you want to connect remotely to . Notice, too, the two in a row closed quotes are now showing where you would add username and password. The local versions are intentionally close quotes because if you used a username and password on the locale connection, an error will occur stating that username and password are not allowed on a local connection.

Security Options

For Impersonation, the options are:

> wbemImpersonationLevelAnonymous = 1
> wbemImpersonationLevelIdentify = 2
> wbemImpersonationLevelImpersonate = 3
> wbemImpersonationLevelDelegate = 4

For Authentication, the options are:

> wbemAuthenticationLevelDefault = 0
> wbemAuthenticationLevelNone = 1
> wbemAuthenticationLevelConnect = 2
> wbemAuthenticationLevelCall = 3
> wbemAuthenticationLevelPkt = 4
> wbemAuthenticationLevelPktIntegrity = 5
> wbemAuthenticationLevelPktPrivacy = 6

Privileges

You can add or remove privileges, too:

> wbemPrivilegeCreateToken = 1
> wbemPrivilegePrimaryToken = 2
> wbemPrivilegeLockMemory = 3
> wbemPrivilegeIncreaseQuota = 4
> wbemPrivilegeMachineAccount = 5
> wbemPrivilegeTcb = 6
> wbemPrivilegeSecurity = 7
> wbemPrivilegeTakeOwnership = 8
> wbemPrivilegeLoadDriver = 9
> wbemPrivilegeSystemProfile =10

```
wbemPrivilegeSystemtime = 11
wbemPrivilegeProfileSingleProcess = 12
wbemPrivilegeIncreaseBasePriority = 13
wbemPrivilegeCreatePagefile = 14
wbemPrivilegeCreatePermanent = 15
wbemPrivilegeBackup = 16
wbemPrivilegeRestore = 17
wbemPrivilegeShutdown = 18
wbemPrivilegeDebug = 19
wbemPrivilegeAudit = 20
wbemPrivilegeSystemEnvironment = 21
wbemPrivilegeChangeNotify = 22
wbemPrivilegeRemoteShutdown = 23
wbemPrivilegeUndock = 24
wbemPrivilegeSyncAgent = 25
wbemPrivilegeEnableDelegation = 26
wbemPrivilegeManageVolume = 27
```

So, the code for using the above may look like this:

```
s.Security_.AuthenticationLevel = wbemAuthenticationLevelPktPrivacy
s.Security_.ImpersonationLevel = wbemImpersonationLevelImpersonate
```

Privileges:

```
s.Security_.Privileges.Add()      one or more of the above
s.Security_.Privileges.Remove()   one or more of the above
```

Okay, now that we've got all the security and privileges out of the way it is time to pull our data back:

Using Get

This is a dual-purpose interface in that it can return information about the class itself and it can return the rows and columns when the object's Instances_() is called:

```
ob = s.Get("Win32_Process", 131027)
```

```
objs = ob.Instances_(0)
```

Using InstancesOf

This interface is best described as the get it done interface.

```
objs = s.InstancesOf("Win32_Process")
```

Using ExecNotificationQuery

Used in line, ExecNotificationQuery enables you to monitor for events you specify in the query:

INSTANCECREATIONEVENT

```
strQuery = "Select * from ___InstanceCreationEvent WITHIN 1 where TargetInstance
ISA 'win32_process'")
        es = s.ExecNotifcationQuery(strQuery)
```

INSTANCEDELETIONEVENT

```
strQuery = "Select * from ___InstanceDeletionEvent WITHIN 1 where TargetInstance
ISA 'win32_process'")
        es = s.ExecNotifcationQuery(strQuery)
```

INSTANCEMODIFICATIONEVENT

```
strQuery = "Select * from ___InstanceModificationEvent WITHIN 1 where
TargetInstance ISA 'win32_process'")
        es = s.ExecNotifcationQuery(strQuery)
```

INSTANCEOPERATIONEVENT

```
strQuery = "Select * from ___InstanceOperationEvent WITHIN 1 where
TargetInstance ISA 'win32_process'")
```

es = s.ExecNotifcationQuery(strQuery)

Using ExecQuery

Used to create standard and custom queries like you would using queries in SQL Server:
Objs = s.ExecQuery("Select * from Win32_Process")

Example of using the Services get Interface

B elow, is an example of using the get interface.

```
import win32com.client
import string
import sys

reload(sys)
sys.setdefaultencoding('UTF8')
def GetValue(prop, obj):
try:
pos = 0
pos1 = 0
Name = str(prop.Name) + " = "
t = ""
s = str(obj.GetObjectText_(0))
pos = s.find(Name)
if pos > 0:
pos = pos + len(prop.Name) + 3
pos1 = len(s)
s = s[pos : pos1]
pos = s.find(";")
s = s[0 : pos]
```

```python
        s = s.replace("{", "")
        s = s.replace("}", "")
        s = s.replace('"', "")
        if len(s) > 12:
        if prop.CIMType == 101:
        t = s[4] + s[5] + '/'
        t = t + s[6] + s[7] + '/'
        t = t + s[0] + s[1] + s[2] + s[3] + " " + s[8] + s[9] + ":" + s[10] + s[11] +':' + s[12] + s[13]
        s = t


        return(s)
        else:
        return("")


        except:
        return("")



        strComputer = "."
        l = win32com.client.Dispatch("WbemScripting.SWbemLocator")
        svc = l.ConnectServer(strComputer,"root\\CIMV2")
        svc.Security_.AuthenticationLevel = 6
        svc.Security_.ImpersonationLevel = 3
        ob = svc.Get("Win32_NetworkLoginProfile")
        objs = ob.Instances_()

        ws = win32com.client.Dispatch("Wscript.Shell")
        fso = win32com.client.Dispatch("Scripting.FileSystemObject")
        txtstream          =          fso.OpenTextFile(ws.CurrentDirectory          +
"\Win32_NetworkLoginProfile", 2, True, -2)
        txtstream.WriteLine("<html>")
        txtstream.WriteLine("<head>")
        txtstream.WriteLine("<title>Win32_NetworkLoginProfile</title>")
        txtstream.WriteLine("</head>")
        txtstream.WriteLine("<body>")
        txtstream.WriteLine("<table cellspacing=2 cellpadding=2>")
```

```
for obj in objs:
txtstream.WriteLine("<tr>")
for prop in obj.Properties_:
txtstream.WriteLine("<th align=left nowrap>" + str(prop.Name) + "</th>")

break

txtstream.WriteLine("</tr>")

for obj in objs:
txtstream.WriteLine("<tr>")
for prop in obj.Properties_:
Value = str(GetValue(prop, obj))
txtstream.WriteLine("<td align=left nowrap>" + Value + "</td>")

txtstream.WriteLine("</tr>")

txtstream.WriteLine("</table>")
txtstream.WriteLine("</body>")
txtstream.WriteLine("</html>")
txtstream.Close
```

Example of using the Services InstancesOf Interface

Below, is an example of using the InstancesOf interface.

```
import win32com.client
import string
import sys

reload(sys)
sys.setdefaultencoding('UTF8')
def GetValue(prop, obj):
try:
pos = 0
pos1 = 0
Name = str(prop.Name) + " = "
t = ""
s = str(obj.GetObjectText_(0))
pos = s.find(Name)
if pos > 0:
pos = pos + len(prop.Name) + 3
pos1 = len(s)
s = s[pos : pos1]
pos = s.find(";")
s = s[0 : pos]
s = s.replace("{", "")
```

```
    s = s.replace("}", "")
    s = s.replace("'", "")
    if len(s) > 12:
    if prop.CIMType == 101:
    t = s[4] + s[5] + '/'
    t = t + s[6] + s[7] + '/'
    t = t + s[0] + s[1] + s[2] + s[3] + " " + s[8] + s[9] + ":" + s[10] + s[11] +':' + s[12] +
s[13]
    s = t


    return(s)
    else:
    return("")


    except:
    return("")


    strComputer = "."
    l = win32com.client.Dispatch("WbemScripting.SWbemLocator")
    svc = l.ConnectServer(strComputer,"root\\CIMV2")
    svc.Security_.AuthenticationLevel = 6
    svc.Security_.ImpersonationLevel = 3
    objs = svc.InstancesOf("Win32_Product")


    ws = win32com.client.Dispatch("Wscript.Shell")
    fso = win32com.client.Dispatch("Scripting.FileSystemObject")
    txtstream = fso.OpenTextFile(ws.CurrentDirectory + "\Win32_Product", 2, True,
-2)
    txtstream.WriteLine("<html>")
    txtstream.WriteLine("<head>")
    txtstream.WriteLine("<title>Win32_Product</title>")
    txtstream.WriteLine("<style type='text/css'>")
    txtstream.WriteLine("th")
    txtstream.WriteLine("{")
    txtstream.WriteLine("    COLOR: white;")
```

```
txtstream.WriteLine("    BACKGROUND-COLOR: navy;")
txtstream.WriteLine("    FONT-FAMILY: Cambria, serif;")
txtstream.WriteLine("    FONT-SIZE: 12px;")
txtstream.WriteLine("    text-align: left;")
txtstream.WriteLine("    white-Space: nowrap;")
txtstream.WriteLine("}")
txtstream.WriteLine("td")
txtstream.WriteLine("{")
txtstream.WriteLine("    COLOR: navy;")
txtstream.WriteLine("    FONT-FAMILY: Cambria, serif;")
txtstream.WriteLine("    FONT-SIZE: 12px;")
txtstream.WriteLine("    text-align: left;")
txtstream.WriteLine("    white-Space: nowrap;")
txtstream.WriteLine("}")
txtstream.WriteLine("div")
txtstream.WriteLine("{")
txtstream.WriteLine("    COLOR: navy;")
txtstream.WriteLine("    FONT-FAMILY: Cambria, serif;")
txtstream.WriteLine("    FONT-SIZE: 12px;")
txtstream.WriteLine("    text-align: left;")
txtstream.WriteLine("    white-Space: nowrap;")
txtstream.WriteLine("}")
txtstream.WriteLine("span")
txtstream.WriteLine("{")
txtstream.WriteLine("    COLOR: navy;")
txtstream.WriteLine("    FONT-FAMILY: Cambria, serif;")
txtstream.WriteLine("    FONT-SIZE: 12px;")
txtstream.WriteLine("    text-align: left;")
txtstream.WriteLine("    white-Space: nowrap;")
txtstream.WriteLine("    width: 100%;")
txtstream.WriteLine("}")
txtstream.WriteLine("textarea")
txtstream.WriteLine("{")
txtstream.WriteLine("    COLOR: navy;")
txtstream.WriteLine("    FONT-FAMILY: Cambria, serif;")
txtstream.WriteLine("    FONT-SIZE: 12px;")
txtstream.WriteLine("    text-align: left;")
txtstream.WriteLine("    white-Space: nowrap;")
txtstream.WriteLine("    display:inline-block;")
txtstream.WriteLine("    width: 100%;")
```

```
txtstream.WriteLine("}")
txtstream.WriteLine("select")
txtstream.WriteLine("{")
txtstream.WriteLine("    COLOR: navy;")
txtstream.WriteLine("    FONT-FAMILY: Cambria, serif;")
txtstream.WriteLine("    FONT-SIZE: 10px;")
txtstream.WriteLine("    text-align: left;")
txtstream.WriteLine("    white-Space: nowrap;")
txtstream.WriteLine("    display:inline-block;")
txtstream.WriteLine("    width: 100%;")
txtstream.WriteLine("}")
txtstream.WriteLine("input")
txtstream.WriteLine("{")
txtstream.WriteLine("    COLOR: navy;")
txtstream.WriteLine("    FONT-FAMILY: Cambria, serif;")
txtstream.WriteLine("    FONT-SIZE: 12px;")
txtstream.WriteLine("    text-align: left;")
txtstream.WriteLine("    display:table-cell;")
txtstream.WriteLine("    white-Space: nowrap;")
txtstream.WriteLine("}")
txtstream.WriteLine("h1 {")
txtstream.WriteLine("color: antiquewhite;")
txtstream.WriteLine("text-shadow: 1px 1px 1px black;")
txtstream.WriteLine("padding: 3px;")
txtstream.WriteLine("text-align: center;")
txtstream.WriteLine("box-shadow: invar 2px 2px 5px rgba(0,0,0,0.5), invar -2px
-2px 5px rgba(255,255,255,0.5)")
txtstream.WriteLine("}")
txtstream.WriteLine("tr:nth-child(even){background-color:#f2f2f2;}")
txtstream.WriteLine("tr:nth-child(odd){background-color:#cccccc;
color:#f2f2f2;}")
txtstream.WriteLine("</style>")
txtstream.WriteLine("</head>")
txtstream.WriteLine("<body>")
txtstream.WriteLine("<table cellspacing=2 cellpadding=2>")
for obj in objs:
txtstream.WriteLine("<tr>")
for prop in obj.Properties_:
txtstream.WriteLine("<th align=left nowrap>" + str(prop.Name) + "</th>")
```

```
break

txtstream.WriteLine("</tr>")

for obj in objs:
txtstream.WriteLine("<tr>")
for prop in obj.Properties_:
Value = str(GetValue(prop, obj))
txtstream.WriteLine("<td align=left nowrap>" + Value + "</td>")

txtstream.WriteLine("</tr>")

txtstream.WriteLine("</table>")
txtstream.WriteLine("</body>")
txtstream.WriteLine("</html>")
txtstream.Close
```

Example of using the Services ExecQuery Interface

Below, are examples of using the ExecQuery Interface.

```
import win32com.client
import string
import sys

reload(sys)
sys.setdefaultencoding('UTF8')
def GetValue(prop, obj):
try:
pos = 0
pos1 = 0
Name = str(prop.Name) + " = "
t = ""
s = str(obj.GetObjectText_(0))
pos = s.find(Name)
if pos > 0:
pos = pos + len(prop.Name) + 3
pos1 = len(s)
s = s[pos : pos1]
pos = s.find(";")
s = s[0 : pos]
s = s.replace("{", "")
```

```
    s = s.replace("}", "")
    s = s.replace("'", "")
    if len(s) > 12:
    if prop.CIMType == 101:
    t = s[4] + s[5] + '/'
    t = t + s[6] + s[7] + '/'
    t = t + s[0] + s[1] + s[2] + s[3] + " " + s[8] + s[9] + ":" + s[10] + s[11] +':' + s[12] +
s[13]
        s = t


    return(s)
    else:
    return("")


    except:
    return("")



    strComputer = "."
    l = win32com.client.Dispatch("WbemScripting.SWbemLocator")
    svc = l.ConnectServer(strComputer,"root\\CIMV2")
    svc.Security_.AuthenticationLevel = 6
    svc.Security_.ImpersonationLevel = 3
    objs = svc.ExecQuery("Select * From Win32_COMClass")


    ws = win32com.client.Dispatch("Wscript.Shell")
    fso = win32com.client.Dispatch("Scripting.FileSystemObject")
    txtstream = fso.OpenTextFile(ws.CurrentDirectory + "\Win32_COMClass", 2,
True, -2)
    txtstream.WriteLine("<html>")
    txtstream.WriteLine("<head>")
    txtstream.WriteLine("<title>Win32_COMClass</title>")
    txtstream.WriteLine("<style type='text/css'>")
    txtstream.WriteLine("th")
    txtstream.WriteLine("{")
    txtstream.WriteLine("    COLOR: white;")
```

```
txtstream.WriteLine("   BACKGROUND-COLOR: navy;")
txtstream.WriteLine("   FONT-FAMILY: Cambria, serif;")
txtstream.WriteLine("   FONT-SIZE: 12px;")
txtstream.WriteLine("   text-align: left;")
txtstream.WriteLine("   white-Space: nowrap;")
txtstream.WriteLine("}")
txtstream.WriteLine("td")
txtstream.WriteLine("{")
txtstream.WriteLine("   COLOR: navy;")
txtstream.WriteLine("   FONT-FAMILY: Cambria, serif;")
txtstream.WriteLine("   FONT-SIZE: 12px;")
txtstream.WriteLine("   text-align: left;")
txtstream.WriteLine("   white-Space: nowrap;")
txtstream.WriteLine("}")
txtstream.WriteLine("div")
txtstream.WriteLine("{")
txtstream.WriteLine("   COLOR: navy;")
txtstream.WriteLine("   FONT-FAMILY: Cambria, serif;")
txtstream.WriteLine("   FONT-SIZE: 12px;")
txtstream.WriteLine("   text-align: left;")
txtstream.WriteLine("   white-Space: nowrap;")
txtstream.WriteLine("}")
txtstream.WriteLine("span")
txtstream.WriteLine("{")
txtstream.WriteLine("   COLOR: navy;")
txtstream.WriteLine("   FONT-FAMILY: Cambria, serif;")
txtstream.WriteLine("   FONT-SIZE: 12px;")
txtstream.WriteLine("   text-align: left;")
txtstream.WriteLine("   white-Space: nowrap;")
txtstream.WriteLine("   width: 100%;")
txtstream.WriteLine("}")
txtstream.WriteLine("textarea")
txtstream.WriteLine("{")
txtstream.WriteLine("   COLOR: navy;")
txtstream.WriteLine("   FONT-FAMILY: Cambria, serif;")
txtstream.WriteLine("   FONT-SIZE: 12px;")
txtstream.WriteLine("   text-align: left;")
txtstream.WriteLine("   white-Space: nowrap;")
txtstream.WriteLine("   display:inline-block;")
txtstream.WriteLine("   width: 100%;")
```

```
txtstream.WriteLine("}")
txtstream.WriteLine("select")
txtstream.WriteLine("{")
txtstream.WriteLine("    COLOR: navy;")
txtstream.WriteLine("    FONT-FAMILY: Cambria, serif;")
txtstream.WriteLine("    FONT-SIZE: 10px;")
txtstream.WriteLine("    text-align: left;")
txtstream.WriteLine("    white-Space: nowrap;")
txtstream.WriteLine("    display:inline-block;")
txtstream.WriteLine("    width: 100%;")
txtstream.WriteLine("}")
txtstream.WriteLine("input")
txtstream.WriteLine("{")
txtstream.WriteLine("    COLOR: navy;")
txtstream.WriteLine("    FONT-FAMILY: Cambria, serif;")
txtstream.WriteLine("    FONT-SIZE: 12px;")
txtstream.WriteLine("    text-align: left;")
txtstream.WriteLine("    display:table-cell;")
txtstream.WriteLine("    white-Space: nowrap;")
txtstream.WriteLine("}")
txtstream.WriteLine("h1 {")
txtstream.WriteLine("color: antiquewhite;")
txtstream.WriteLine("text-shadow: 1px 1px 1px black;")
txtstream.WriteLine("padding: 3px;")
txtstream.WriteLine("text-align: center;")
txtstream.WriteLine("box-shadow: invar 2px 2px 5px rgba(0,0,0,0.5), invar -2px
-2px 5px rgba(255,255,255,0.5)")
txtstream.WriteLine("}")
txtstream.WriteLine("tr:nth-child(even){background-color:#f2f2f2;}")
txtstream.WriteLine("tr:nth-child(odd){background-color:#cccccc;
color:#f2f2f2;}")
txtstream.WriteLine("</style>")
txtstream.WriteLine("</head>")
txtstream.WriteLine("<body>")
txtstream.WriteLine("<table cellspacing=2 cellpadding=2>")
for obj in objs:
txtstream.WriteLine("<tr>")
for prop in obj.Properties_:
txtstream.WriteLine("<th align=left nowrap>" + str(prop.Name) + "</th>")
```

```
break

txtstream.WriteLine("</tr>")

for obj in objs:
txtstream.WriteLine("<tr>")
for prop in obj.Properties_:
Value = str(GetValue(prop, obj))
txtstream.WriteLine("<td align=left nowrap>" + Value + "</td>")

txtstream.WriteLine("</tr>")

txtstream.WriteLine("</table>")
txtstream.WriteLine("</body>")
txtstream.WriteLine("</html>")
txtstream.Close
```

Example of using the Services ExecNotificationQuery Interface

B elow, are examples of using the ExecNotificationQuery interface.

InstanceCreationEvent

```
import win32com.client
import string
import sys

reload(sys)
sys.setdefaultencoding('UTF8')
def GetValue(prop, obj):
try:
pos = 0
pos1 = 0
Name = str(prop.Name) + " = "
t = ""
s = str(obj.GetObjectText_(0))
pos = s.find(Name)
if pos > 0:
pos = pos + len(prop.Name) + 3
```

```python
    pos1 = len(s)
    s = s[pos : pos1]
    pos = s.find(";")
    s = s[0 : pos]
    s = s.replace("{", "")
    s = s.replace("}", "")
    s = s.replace('"', "")
    if len(s) > 12:
    if prop.CIMType == 101:
    t = s[4] + s[5] + '/'
    t = t + s[6] + s[7] + '/'
    t = t + s[0] + s[1] + s[2] + s[3] + " " + s[8] + s[9] + ":" + s[10] + s[11] +':' + s[12] +
s[13]
    s = t


    return(s)
    else:
    return("")


    except:
    return("")


    strComputer = "."
    l = win32com.client.Dispatch("WbemScripting.SWbemLocator")
    svc = l.ConnectServer(strComputer,"root\\CIMV2")
    svc.Security_.AuthenticationLevel = 6
    svc.Security_.ImpersonationLevel = 3
    es = svc.ExecNotificationQuery("Select  *  From  ___InstanceCreationEvent
WITHIN 1 where TargetInstance ISA'Win32_Process'")

    v=0
    ws = win32com.client.Dispatch("Wscript.Shell")
    fso = win32com.client.Dispatch("Scripting.FileSystemObject")
    txtstream = fso.OpenTextFile(ws.CurrentDirectory + "\Win32_Process", 2, True,
-2)
    txtstream.WriteLine("<html>")
```

```
txtstream.WriteLine("<head>")
txtstream.WriteLine("<title>Win32_Process</title>")
txtstream.WriteLine("<style type='text/css'>")
txtstream.WriteLine("th")
txtstream.WriteLine("{")
txtstream.WriteLine("    COLOR: white;")
txtstream.WriteLine("    BACKGROUND-COLOR: navy;")
txtstream.WriteLine("    FONT-FAMILY: Cambria, serif;")
txtstream.WriteLine("    FONT-SIZE: 12px;")
txtstream.WriteLine("    text-align: left;")
txtstream.WriteLine("    white-Space: nowrap;")
txtstream.WriteLine("}")
txtstream.WriteLine("td")
txtstream.WriteLine("{")
txtstream.WriteLine("    COLOR: navy;")
txtstream.WriteLine("    FONT-FAMILY: Cambria, serif;")
txtstream.WriteLine("    FONT-SIZE: 12px;")
txtstream.WriteLine("    text-align: left;")
txtstream.WriteLine("    white-Space: nowrap;")
txtstream.WriteLine("}")
txtstream.WriteLine("div")
txtstream.WriteLine("{")
txtstream.WriteLine("    COLOR: navy;")
txtstream.WriteLine("    FONT-FAMILY: Cambria, serif;")
txtstream.WriteLine("    FONT-SIZE: 12px;")
txtstream.WriteLine("    text-align: left;")
txtstream.WriteLine("    white-Space: nowrap;")
txtstream.WriteLine("}")
txtstream.WriteLine("span")
txtstream.WriteLine("{")
txtstream.WriteLine("    COLOR: navy;")
txtstream.WriteLine("    FONT-FAMILY: Cambria, serif;")
txtstream.WriteLine("    FONT-SIZE: 12px;")
txtstream.WriteLine("    text-align: left;")
txtstream.WriteLine("    white-Space: nowrap;")
txtstream.WriteLine("    width: 100%;")
txtstream.WriteLine("}")
txtstream.WriteLine("textarea")
txtstream.WriteLine("{")
txtstream.WriteLine("    COLOR: navy;")
```

```
txtstream.WriteLine("    FONT-FAMILY: Cambria, serif;")
txtstream.WriteLine("    FONT-SIZE: 12px;")
txtstream.WriteLine("    text-align: left;")
txtstream.WriteLine("    white-Space: nowrap;")
txtstream.WriteLine("    display:inline-block;")
txtstream.WriteLine("    width: 100%;")
txtstream.WriteLine("}")
txtstream.WriteLine("select")
txtstream.WriteLine("{")
txtstream.WriteLine("    COLOR: navy;")
txtstream.WriteLine("    FONT-FAMILY: Cambria, serif;")
txtstream.WriteLine("    FONT-SIZE: 10px;")
txtstream.WriteLine("    text-align: left;")
txtstream.WriteLine("    white-Space: nowrap;")
txtstream.WriteLine("    display:inline-block;")
txtstream.WriteLine("    width: 100%;")
txtstream.WriteLine("}")
txtstream.WriteLine("input")
txtstream.WriteLine("{")
txtstream.WriteLine("    COLOR: navy;")
txtstream.WriteLine("    FONT-FAMILY: Cambria, serif;")
txtstream.WriteLine("    FONT-SIZE: 12px;")
txtstream.WriteLine("    text-align: left;")
txtstream.WriteLine("    display:table-cell;")
txtstream.WriteLine("    white-Space: nowrap;")
txtstream.WriteLine("}")
txtstream.WriteLine("h1 {")
txtstream.WriteLine("color: antiquewhite;")
txtstream.WriteLine("text-shadow: 1px 1px 1px black;")
txtstream.WriteLine("padding: 3px;")
txtstream.WriteLine("text-align: center;")
txtstream.WriteLine("box-shadow: invar 2px 2px 5px rgba(0,0,0,0.5), invar -2px
-2px 5px rgba(255,255,255,0.5)")
txtstream.WriteLine("}")
txtstream.WriteLine("tr:nth-child(even){background-color:#f2f2f2;}")
txtstream.WriteLine("tr:nth-child(odd){background-color:#cccccc;
color:#f2f2f2;}")
txtstream.WriteLine("</style>")
txtstream.WriteLine("</head>")
txtstream.WriteLine("<body>")
```

```
txtstream.WriteLine("<table cellspacing=2 cellpadding=2>")
while v < 5:
ti = es.NextEvent(-1)
obj = ti.Properties_.Item("TargetInstance").Value
if v == 0:
txtstream.WriteLine("<tr>")
for prop in obj.Properties_:
txtstream.WriteLine("<th align=left nowrap>" + str(prop.Name) + "</th>")

txtstream.WriteLine("</tr>")

txtstream.WriteLine("<tr>")
for prop in obj.Properties_:
Value = str(GetValue(prop, obj))
txtstream.WriteLine("<td align=left nowrap>" + Value + "</td>")

txtstream.WriteLine("</tr>")
v=v+1

txtstream.WriteLine("</table>")
txtstream.WriteLine("</body>")
txtstream.WriteLine("</html>")
txtstream.Close
```

InstanceDeletionEvent

```
import win32com.client
import string
import sys

reload(sys)
sys.setdefaultencoding('UTF8')
def GetValue(prop, obj):
try:
pos = 0
pos1 = 0
Name = str(prop.Name) + " = "
t = ""
s = str(obj.GetObjectText_(0))
```

```python
    pos = s.find(Name)
    if pos > 0:
    pos = pos + len(prop.Name) + 3
    pos1 = len(s)
    s = s[pos : pos1]
    pos = s.find(";")
    s = s[0 : pos]
    s = s.replace("{", "")
    s = s.replace("}", "")
    s = s.replace('"', "")
    if len(s) > 12:
    if prop.CIMType == 101:
    t = s[4] + s[5] + '/'
    t = t + s[6] + s[7] + '/'
    t = t + s[0] + s[1] + s[2] + s[3] + " " + s[8] + s[9] + ":" + s[10] + s[11] +':' + s[12] +
s[13]
    s = t


    return(s)
    else:
    return("")



    except:
    return("")



    strComputer = "."
    l = win32com.client.Dispatch("WbemScripting.SWbemLocator")
    svc = l.ConnectServer(strComputer,"root\\CIMV2")
    svc.Security_.AuthenticationLevel = 6
    svc.Security_.ImpersonationLevel = 3
    es  =  svc.ExecNotificationQuery("Select  *  From  ___InstanceDeletionEvent
WITHIN 1 where TargetInstance ISA'Win32_Process'")

    v=0
    ws = win32com.client.Dispatch("Wscript.Shell")
    fso = win32com.client.Dispatch("Scripting.FileSystemObject")
```

```
txtstream = fso.OpenTextFile(ws.CurrentDirectory + "\Win32_Process", 2, True,
-2)
    txtstream.WriteLine("<html>")
    txtstream.WriteLine("<head>")
    txtstream.WriteLine("<title>Win32_Process</title>")
    txtstream.WriteLine("<style type='text/css'>")
    txtstream.WriteLine("th")
    txtstream.WriteLine("{")
    txtstream.WriteLine("   COLOR: white;")
    txtstream.WriteLine("   BACKGROUND-COLOR: navy;")
    txtstream.WriteLine("   FONT-FAMILY: Cambria, serif;")
    txtstream.WriteLine("   FONT-SIZE: 12px;")
    txtstream.WriteLine("   text-align: left;")
    txtstream.WriteLine("   white-Space: nowrap;")
    txtstream.WriteLine("}")
    txtstream.WriteLine("td")
    txtstream.WriteLine("{")
    txtstream.WriteLine("   COLOR: navy;")
    txtstream.WriteLine("   FONT-FAMILY: Cambria, serif;")
    txtstream.WriteLine("   FONT-SIZE: 12px;")
    txtstream.WriteLine("   text-align: left;")
    txtstream.WriteLine("   white-Space: nowrap;")
    txtstream.WriteLine("}")
    txtstream.WriteLine("div")
    txtstream.WriteLine("{")
    txtstream.WriteLine("   COLOR: navy;")
    txtstream.WriteLine("   FONT-FAMILY: Cambria, serif;")
    txtstream.WriteLine("   FONT-SIZE: 12px;")
    txtstream.WriteLine("   text-align: left;")
    txtstream.WriteLine("   white-Space: nowrap;")
    txtstream.WriteLine("}")
    txtstream.WriteLine("span")
    txtstream.WriteLine("{")
    txtstream.WriteLine("   COLOR: navy;")
    txtstream.WriteLine("   FONT-FAMILY: Cambria, serif;")
    txtstream.WriteLine("   FONT-SIZE: 12px;")
    txtstream.WriteLine("   text-align: left;")
    txtstream.WriteLine("   white-Space: nowrap;")
    txtstream.WriteLine("   width: 100%;")
    txtstream.WriteLine("}")
```

```
txtstream.WriteLine("textarea")
txtstream.WriteLine("{")
txtstream.WriteLine("   COLOR: navy;")
txtstream.WriteLine("   FONT-FAMILY: Cambria, serif;")
txtstream.WriteLine("   FONT-SIZE: 12px;")
txtstream.WriteLine("   text-align: left;")
txtstream.WriteLine("   white-Space: nowrap;")
txtstream.WriteLine("   display:inline-block;")
txtstream.WriteLine("   width: 100%;")
txtstream.WriteLine("}")
txtstream.WriteLine("select")
txtstream.WriteLine("{")
txtstream.WriteLine("   COLOR: navy;")
txtstream.WriteLine("   FONT-FAMILY: Cambria, serif;")
txtstream.WriteLine("   FONT-SIZE: 10px;")
txtstream.WriteLine("   text-align: left;")
txtstream.WriteLine("   white-Space: nowrap;")
txtstream.WriteLine("   display:inline-block;")
txtstream.WriteLine("   width: 100%;")
txtstream.WriteLine("}")
txtstream.WriteLine("input")
txtstream.WriteLine("{")
txtstream.WriteLine("   COLOR: navy;")
txtstream.WriteLine("   FONT-FAMILY: Cambria, serif;")
txtstream.WriteLine("   FONT-SIZE: 12px;")
txtstream.WriteLine("   text-align: left;")
txtstream.WriteLine("   display:table-cell;")
txtstream.WriteLine("   white-Space: nowrap;")
txtstream.WriteLine("}")
txtstream.WriteLine("h1 {")
txtstream.WriteLine("color: antiquewhite;")
txtstream.WriteLine("text-shadow: 1px 1px 1px black;")
txtstream.WriteLine("padding: 3px;")
txtstream.WriteLine("text-align: center;")
txtstream.WriteLine("box-shadow: invar 2px 2px 5px rgba(0,0,0,0.5), invar -2px
-2px 5px rgba(255,255,255,0.5)")
txtstream.WriteLine("}")
txtstream.WriteLine("tr:nth-child(even){background-color:#f2f2f2;}")
txtstream.WriteLine("tr:nth-child(odd){background-color:#cccccc;
color:#f2f2f2;}")
```

```
txtstream.WriteLine("</style>")
txtstream.WriteLine("</head>")
txtstream.WriteLine("<body>")
txtstream.WriteLine("<table cellspacing=2 cellpadding=2>")
while v < 5:
ti = es.NextEvent(-1)
obj = ti.Properties_.Item("TargetInstance").Value
if v == 0:
txtstream.WriteLine("<tr>")
for prop in obj.Properties_:
txtstream.WriteLine("<th align=left nowrap>" + str(prop.Name) + "</th>")

txtstream.WriteLine("</tr>")

txtstream.WriteLine("<tr>")
for prop in obj.Properties_:
Value = str(GetValue(prop, obj))
txtstream.WriteLine("<td align=left nowrap>" + Value + "</td>")

txtstream.WriteLine("</tr>")
v=v+1

txtstream.WriteLine("</table>")
txtstream.WriteLine("</body>")
txtstream.WriteLine("</html>")
txtstream.Close
```

InstanceModificationEvent

```
import win32com.client
import string
import sys

reload(sys)
sys.setdefaultencoding('UTF8')
def GetValue(prop, obj):
try:
pos = 0
pos1 = 0
```

```python
    Name = str(prop.Name) + " = "
    t = ""
    s = str(obj.GetObjectText_(0))
    pos = s.find(Name)
    if pos > 0:
    pos = pos + len(prop.Name) + 3
    pos1 = len(s)
    s = s[pos : pos1]
    pos = s.find(";")
    s = s[0 : pos]
    s = s.replace("{", "")
    s = s.replace("}", "")
    s = s.replace('"', "")
    if len(s) > 12:
    if prop.CIMType == 101:
    t = s[4] + s[5] + '/'
    t = t + s[6] + s[7] + '/'
    t = t + s[0] + s[1] + s[2] + s[3] + " " + s[8] + s[9] + ":" + s[10] + s[11] +':' + s[12] +
s[13]
    s = t


    return(s)
    else:
    return("")


    except:
    return("")



    strComputer = "."
    l = win32com.client.Dispatch("WbemScripting.SWbemLocator")
    svc = l.ConnectServer(strComputer,"root\\CIMV2")
    svc.Security_.AuthenticationLevel = 6
    svc.Security_.ImpersonationLevel = 3
    es = svc.ExecNotificationQuery("Select  *  From  ___InstanceModificationEvent
WITHIN 1 where TargetInstance ISA'Win32_Process'")
```

```
v=0
ws = win32com.client.Dispatch("Wscript.Shell")
fso = win32com.client.Dispatch("Scripting.FileSystemObject")
txtstream = fso.OpenTextFile(ws.CurrentDirectory + "\Win32_Process", 2, True,
-2)
txtstream.WriteLine("<html>")
txtstream.WriteLine("<head>")
txtstream.WriteLine("<title>Win32_Process</title>")
txtstream.WriteLine("<style type='text/css'>")
txtstream.WriteLine("th")
txtstream.WriteLine("{")
txtstream.WriteLine("   COLOR: white;")
txtstream.WriteLine("   BACKGROUND-COLOR: navy;")
txtstream.WriteLine("   FONT-FAMILY: Cambria, serif;")
txtstream.WriteLine("   FONT-SIZE: 12px;")
txtstream.WriteLine("   text-align: left;")
txtstream.WriteLine("   white-Space: nowrap;")
txtstream.WriteLine("}")
txtstream.WriteLine("td")
txtstream.WriteLine("{")
txtstream.WriteLine("   COLOR: navy;")
txtstream.WriteLine("   FONT-FAMILY: Cambria, serif;")
txtstream.WriteLine("   FONT-SIZE: 12px;")
txtstream.WriteLine("   text-align: left;")
txtstream.WriteLine("   white-Space: nowrap;")
txtstream.WriteLine("}")
txtstream.WriteLine("div")
txtstream.WriteLine("{")
txtstream.WriteLine("   COLOR: navy;")
txtstream.WriteLine("   FONT-FAMILY: Cambria, serif;")
txtstream.WriteLine("   FONT-SIZE: 12px;")
txtstream.WriteLine("   text-align: left;")
txtstream.WriteLine("   white-Space: nowrap;")
txtstream.WriteLine("}")
txtstream.WriteLine("span")
txtstream.WriteLine("{")
txtstream.WriteLine("   COLOR: navy;")
txtstream.WriteLine("   FONT-FAMILY: Cambria, serif;")
txtstream.WriteLine("   FONT-SIZE: 12px;")
txtstream.WriteLine("   text-align: left;")
```

```
txtstream.WriteLine("    white-Space: nowrap;")
txtstream.WriteLine("    width: 100%;")
txtstream.WriteLine("}")
txtstream.WriteLine("textarea")
txtstream.WriteLine("{")
txtstream.WriteLine("    COLOR: navy;")
txtstream.WriteLine("    FONT-FAMILY: Cambria, serif;")
txtstream.WriteLine("    FONT-SIZE: 12px;")
txtstream.WriteLine("    text-align: left;")
txtstream.WriteLine("    white-Space: nowrap;")
txtstream.WriteLine("    display:inline-block;")
txtstream.WriteLine("    width: 100%;")
txtstream.WriteLine("}")
txtstream.WriteLine("select")
txtstream.WriteLine("{")
txtstream.WriteLine("    COLOR: navy;")
txtstream.WriteLine("    FONT-FAMILY: Cambria, serif;")
txtstream.WriteLine("    FONT-SIZE: 10px;")
txtstream.WriteLine("    text-align: left;")
txtstream.WriteLine("    white-Space: nowrap;")
txtstream.WriteLine("    display:inline-block;")
txtstream.WriteLine("    width: 100%;")
txtstream.WriteLine("}")
txtstream.WriteLine("input")
txtstream.WriteLine("{")
txtstream.WriteLine("    COLOR: navy;")
txtstream.WriteLine("    FONT-FAMILY: Cambria, serif;")
txtstream.WriteLine("    FONT-SIZE: 12px;")
txtstream.WriteLine("    text-align: left;")
txtstream.WriteLine("    display:table-cell;")
txtstream.WriteLine("    white-Space: nowrap;")
txtstream.WriteLine("}")
txtstream.WriteLine("h1 {")
txtstream.WriteLine("color: antiquewhite;")
txtstream.WriteLine("text-shadow: 1px 1px 1px black;")
txtstream.WriteLine("padding: 3px;")
txtstream.WriteLine("text-align: center;")
txtstream.WriteLine("box-shadow: invar 2px 2px 5px rgba(0,0,0,0.5), invar -2px
-2px 5px rgba(255,255,255,0.5)")
txtstream.WriteLine("}")
```

```
txtstream.WriteLine("tr:nth-child(even){background-color:#f2f2f2;}")
txtstream.WriteLine("tr:nth-child(odd){background-color:#cccccc;
color:#f2f2f2;}")
txtstream.WriteLine("</style>")
txtstream.WriteLine("</head>")
txtstream.WriteLine("<body>")
txtstream.WriteLine("<table cellspacing=2 cellpadding=2>")
while v < 5:
ti = es.NextEvent(-1)
obj = ti.Properties_.Item("TargetInstance").Value
if v == 0:
txtstream.WriteLine("<tr>")
for prop in obj.Properties_:
txtstream.WriteLine("<th align=left nowrap>" + str(prop.Name) + "</th>")

txtstream.WriteLine("</tr>")

txtstream.WriteLine("<tr>")
for prop in obj.Properties_:
Value = str(GetValue(prop, obj))
txtstream.WriteLine("<td align=left nowrap>" + Value + "</td>")

txtstream.WriteLine("</tr>")
v=v+1

txtstream.WriteLine("</table>")
txtstream.WriteLine("</body>")
txtstream.WriteLine("</html>")
txtstream.Close
```

InstanceOperationEvent

```
import win32com.client
import string
import sys

reload(sys)
sys.setdefaultencoding('UTF8')
def GetValue(prop, obj):
```

```
try:
pos = 0
pos1 = 0
Name = str(prop.Name) + " = "
t = ""
s = str(obj.GetObjectText_(0))
pos = s.find(Name)
if pos > 0:
pos = pos + len(prop.Name) + 3
pos1 = len(s)
s = s[pos : pos1]
pos = s.find(";")
s = s[0 : pos]
s = s.replace("{", "")
s = s.replace("}", "")
s = s.replace('"', "")
if len(s) > 12:
if prop.CIMType == 101:
t = s[4] + s[5] + '/'
t = t + s[6] + s[7] + '/'
t = t + s[0] + s[1] + s[2] + s[3] + " " + s[8] + s[9] + ":" + s[10] + s[11] +':' + s[12] +
s[13]
s = t


return(s)
else:
return("")


except:
return("")


strComputer = "."
l = win32com.client.Dispatch("WbemScripting.SWbemLocator")
svc = l.ConnectServer(strComputer,"root\\CIMV2")
svc.Security_.AuthenticationLevel = 6
svc.Security_.ImpersonationLevel = 3
```

```
    es = svc.ExecNotificationQuery("Select * From ___InstanceOperationEvent
WITHIN 1 where TargetInstance ISA'Win32_Process'")

    v=0
    ws = win32com.client.Dispatch("Wscript.Shell")
    fso = win32com.client.Dispatch("Scripting.FileSystemObject")
    txtstream = fso.OpenTextFile(ws.CurrentDirectory + "\Win32_Process", 2, True,
-2)
    txtstream.WriteLine("<html>")
    txtstream.WriteLine("<head>")
    txtstream.WriteLine("<title>Win32_Process</title>")
    txtstream.WriteLine("<style type='text/css'>")
    txtstream.WriteLine("th")
    txtstream.WriteLine("{")
    txtstream.WriteLine("   COLOR: white;")
    txtstream.WriteLine("   BACKGROUND-COLOR: navy;")
    txtstream.WriteLine("   FONT-FAMILY: Cambria, serif;")
    txtstream.WriteLine("   FONT-SIZE: 12px;")
    txtstream.WriteLine("   text-align: left;")
    txtstream.WriteLine("   white-Space: nowrap;")
    txtstream.WriteLine("}")
    txtstream.WriteLine("td")
    txtstream.WriteLine("{")
    txtstream.WriteLine("   COLOR: navy;")
    txtstream.WriteLine("   FONT-FAMILY: Cambria, serif;")
    txtstream.WriteLine("   FONT-SIZE: 12px;")
    txtstream.WriteLine("   text-align: left;")
    txtstream.WriteLine("   white-Space: nowrap;")
    txtstream.WriteLine("}")
    txtstream.WriteLine("div")
    txtstream.WriteLine("{")
    txtstream.WriteLine("   COLOR: navy;")
    txtstream.WriteLine("   FONT-FAMILY: Cambria, serif;")
    txtstream.WriteLine("   FONT-SIZE: 12px;")
    txtstream.WriteLine("   text-align: left;")
    txtstream.WriteLine("   white-Space: nowrap;")
    txtstream.WriteLine("}")
    txtstream.WriteLine("span")
    txtstream.WriteLine("{")
    txtstream.WriteLine("   COLOR: navy;")
```

```
txtstream.WriteLine("    FONT-FAMILY: Cambria, serif;")
txtstream.WriteLine("    FONT-SIZE: 12px;")
txtstream.WriteLine("    text-align: left;")
txtstream.WriteLine("    white-Space: nowrap;")
txtstream.WriteLine("    width: 100%;")
txtstream.WriteLine("}")
txtstream.WriteLine("textarea")
txtstream.WriteLine("{")
txtstream.WriteLine("    COLOR: navy;")
txtstream.WriteLine("    FONT-FAMILY: Cambria, serif;")
txtstream.WriteLine("    FONT-SIZE: 12px;")
txtstream.WriteLine("    text-align: left;")
txtstream.WriteLine("    white-Space: nowrap;")
txtstream.WriteLine("    display:inline-block;")
txtstream.WriteLine("    width: 100%;")
txtstream.WriteLine("}")
txtstream.WriteLine("select")
txtstream.WriteLine("{")
txtstream.WriteLine("    COLOR: navy;")
txtstream.WriteLine("    FONT-FAMILY: Cambria, serif;")
txtstream.WriteLine("    FONT-SIZE: 10px;")
txtstream.WriteLine("    text-align: left;")
txtstream.WriteLine("    white-Space: nowrap;")
txtstream.WriteLine("    display:inline-block;")
txtstream.WriteLine("    width: 100%;")
txtstream.WriteLine("}")
txtstream.WriteLine("input")
txtstream.WriteLine("{")
txtstream.WriteLine("    COLOR: navy;")
txtstream.WriteLine("    FONT-FAMILY: Cambria, serif;")
txtstream.WriteLine("    FONT-SIZE: 12px;")
txtstream.WriteLine("    text-align: left;")
txtstream.WriteLine("    display:table-cell;")
txtstream.WriteLine("    white-Space: nowrap;")
txtstream.WriteLine("}")
txtstream.WriteLine("h1 {")
txtstream.WriteLine("color: antiquewhite;")
txtstream.WriteLine("text-shadow: 1px 1px 1px black;")
txtstream.WriteLine("padding: 3px;")
txtstream.WriteLine("text-align: center;")
```

```
txtstream.WriteLine("box-shadow: invar 2px 2px 5px rgba(0,0,0,0.5), invar -2px
-2px 5px rgba(255,255,255,0.5)")
txtstream.WriteLine("}")
txtstream.WriteLine("tr:nth-child(even){background-color:#f2f2f2;}")
txtstream.WriteLine("tr:nth-child(odd){background-color:#cccccc;
color:#f2f2f2;}")
txtstream.WriteLine("</style>")
txtstream.WriteLine("</head>")
txtstream.WriteLine("<body>")
txtstream.WriteLine("<table cellspacing=2 cellpadding=2>")
while v < 5:
ti = es.NextEvent(-1)
obj = ti.Properties_.Item("TargetInstance").Value
if v == 0:
txtstream.WriteLine("<tr>")
for prop in obj.Properties_:
txtstream.WriteLine("<th align=left nowrap>" + str(prop.Name) + "</th>")

txtstream.WriteLine("</tr>")

txtstream.WriteLine("<tr>")
for prop in obj.Properties_:
Value = str(GetValue(prop, obj))
txtstream.WriteLine("<td align=left nowrap>" + Value + "</td>")

txtstream.WriteLine("</tr>")
v=v+1

txtstream.WriteLine("</table>")
txtstream.WriteLine("</body>")
txtstream.WriteLine("</html>")
txtstream.Close
```

Access was never this easy
30 minutes could make you hundreds

*When a person doesn't want to listen to what you
have to say, chains and shackles are on their way.*
--R. T. Edwards

Atfirst glance, something as big as Access ought to be hard to work with. Truth is, nothing could be farther from the truth and yes, I am wasting no time on the usual ego massage on either side of the e-book.
Please look at the following code:

Create Access

```
import win32com.client


oAccess = win32com.client.Dispatch("Access.Application")
oAccess.Visible = true
```

Create an Access 2000 Database

```
oAccess.NewCurrentDatabase(Path + "\\" + DBName + ".mdb", 9)
```

Create an Access 2002 Database

```
oAccess.NewCurrentDatabase(Path + "\\" + DBName + ".mdb", 10)
```

Create an Access 2007 database

```
oAccess.NewCurrentDatabase(Path + "\\" + DBName + ".accdb", 12)
```

Create an Access Default Database

```
oAccess.NewCurrentDatabase(Path + "\\" + DBName + ".accdb", 0)

OAccess.Quit
```

Open an Access Database

```
import win32com.client

oAccess = win32com.client.Dispatch("Access.Application")
oAccess.Visible = true
oAccess.OpenCurrentDatabase(Path + "\\" + DBName + ".mdb")
```

or:

```
oAccess.OpenCurrentDatabase(Path + "\\" + DBName + ".accdb")
```

Putting it all together

```
import win32com.client
```

```python
import string
import sys

reload(sys)
sys.setdefaultencoding('UTF8')
def GetValue(prop, obj):
try:
pos = 0
pos1 = 0
Name = str(prop.Name) + " = "
t = ""
s = str(obj.GetObjectText_(0))
pos = s.find(Name)
if pos > 0:
pos = pos + len(prop.Name) + 3
pos1 = len(s)
s = s[pos : pos1]
pos = s.find(";")
s = s[0 : pos]
s = s.replace("{", "")
s = s.replace("}", "")
s = s.replace("'", "")
if len(s) > 12:
if prop.CIMType == 101:
t = s[4] + s[5] + '/'
t = t + s[6] + s[7] + '/'
t = t + s[0] + s[1] + s[2] + s[3] + " " + s[8] + s[9] + ":" + s[10] + s[11] +':' + s[12] +
s[13]
s = t


return(s)
else:
return("")


except:
return("")
```

```
strComputer = "."
l = win32com.client.Dispatch("WbemScripting.SWbemLocator")
svc = l.ConnectServer(strComputer,"root\\CIMV2")
svc.Security_.AuthenticationLevel = 6
svc.Security_.ImpersonationLevel = 3
objs = svc.ExecQuery("Select * From Win32_COMClass")


oAccess =  win32com.client.Dispatch("Access.Application")
oAccess.NewCurrentDatabase("D:\\COMClasses.accdb", 12)

db = oAccess.CurrentDB()
tbldef = db.CreateTableDef("COMClass")
for obj in objs:
for prop in obj.Properties_:
fld = tbldef.CreateField(prop.Name, 12)
fld.AllowZeroLength = True
tbldef.Fields.Append(fld)

break

db.TableDefs.Append(tbldef)

rs = db.OpenRecordset("COMClass")
for obj in objs:
rs.AddNew()
for prop in obj.Properties_:
rs.Fields(prop.Name).Value = GetValue(prop, obj)

rs.Update()
```

Creating XML Files

Attribute XML

I may not be rich, but my children are my biggest
asset.
—*R. T. Edwards*

Whatis attribute XML? This one always gets me in hot water.
Why?
Because, technically any element formatted XML could also be considered Attribute XML with an Element tag. Technically, Attribute XML is one or more name and values contained within a single node.

Attribute XML

```
import win32com.client
import string
import sys

reload(sys)
sys.setdefaultencoding('UTF8')
def GetValue(prop, obj):
try:
pos = 0
```

```python
        pos1 = 0
        Name = str(prop.Name) + " = "
        t = ""
        s = str(obj.GetObjectText_(0))
        pos = s.find(Name)
        if pos > 0:
            pos = pos + len(prop.Name) + 3
            pos1 = len(s)
            s = s[pos : pos1]
            pos = s.find(";")
            s = s[0 : pos]
            s = s.replace("{", "")
            s = s.replace("}", "")
            s = s.replace('"', "")
            if len(s) > 12:
                if prop.CIMType == 101:
                    t = s[4] + s[5] + '/'
                    t = t + s[6] + s[7] + '/'
                    t = t + s[0] + s[1] + s[2] + s[3] + " " + s[8] + s[9] + ":" + s[10] + s[11] +':' + s[12] + s[13]
                    s = t


            return(s)
        else:
            return("")


    except:
        return("")




strComputer = "."
l = win32com.client.Dispatch("WbemScripting.SWbemLocator")
svc = l.ConnectServer(strComputer,"root\\CIMV2")
svc.Security_.AuthenticationLevel = 6
svc.Security_.ImpersonationLevel = 3
objs = svc.ExecQuery("Select * From Win32_Process")
```

```
xmldoc = win32com.client.Dispatch("MSXML2.DOMDocument")
pi = xmldoc.CreateProcessingInstruction("xml", "version='1.0' encoding='ISO-8859-1'")
oRoot = xmldoc.CreateElement("data")
xmldoc.AppendChild(pi)
for obj in objs:
oNode = xmldoc.CreateNode(1, "Win32_Process", "")
for prop in obj.Properties_:
oNode1 = xmldoc.CreateElement(Prop.Name)
onode1.InnerText = GetValue(prop, obj)
oNode.AppendChild(oNode1)

oRoot.AppendChild(oNode)

xmldoc.AppendChild(oRoot)
ws = win32com.client.Dispatch("WScript.Shell")
xmldoc.Save(ws.CurrentDirectory + "\\Win32_Process.xml")
```

Element XML

```
import win32com.client
import string
import sys

reload(sys)
sys.setdefaultencoding('UTF8')
def GetValue(prop, obj):
try:
pos = 0
pos1 = 0
Name = str(prop.Name) + " = "
t = ""
s = str(obj.GetObjectText_(0))
pos = s.find(Name)
if pos > 0:
pos = pos + len(prop.Name) + 3
```

```python
        pos1 = len(s)
        s = s[pos : pos1]
        pos = s.find(";")
        s = s[0 : pos]
        s = s.replace("{", "")
        s = s.replace("}", "")
        s = s.replace('"', "")
        if len(s) > 12:
        if prop.CIMType == 101:
        t = s[4] + s[5] + '/'
        t = t + s[6] + s[7] + '/'
        t = t + s[0] + s[1] + s[2] + s[3] + " " + s[8] + s[9] + ":" + s[10] + s[11] +':' + s[12]
+ s[13]
        s = t


        return(s)
        else:
        return("")


        except:
        return("")




        strComputer = "."
        l = win32com.client.Dispatch("WbemScripting.SWbemLocator")
        svc = l.ConnectServer(strComputer,"root\\CIMV2")
        svc.Security_.AuthenticationLevel = 6
        svc.Security_.ImpersonationLevel = 3
        objs = svc.ExecQuery("Select * From Win32_Process")
```

```
xmldoc  = win32com.client.Dispatch("MSXML2.DOMDocument")
pi = xmldoc.CreateProcessingInstruction("xml", "version='1.0' encoding='ISO-
8859-1'")
oRoot = xmldoc.CreateElement("data")
xmldoc.AppendChild(pi)
for obj in objs:
oNode = xmldoc.CreateElement("Win32_Process")
for prop in obj.Properties_:
oNode1 = xmldoc.CreateElement(prop.Name)
oNode1.Text = GetValue(prop, obj)
oNode.AppendChild(oNode1)

oRoot.AppendChild(oNode)

xmldoc.AppendChild(oRoot)
ws = win32com.client.Dispatch("WScript.Shell")
xmldoc.Save(ws.CurrentDirectory + "\\Process.xml")
```

Element XML For XSL

```
import win32com.client
import string
import sys

reload(sys)
sys.setdefaultencoding('UTF8')
def GetValue(prop, obj):
try:
pos = 0
pos1 = 0
Name = str(prop.Name) + " = "
```

```python
        t = ""
        s = str(obj.GetObjectText_(0))
        pos = s.find(Name)
        if pos > 0:
        pos = pos + len(prop.Name) + 3
        pos1 = len(s)
        s = s[pos : pos1]
        pos = s.find(";")
        s = s[0 : pos]
        s = s.replace("{", "")
        s = s.replace("}", "")
        s = s.replace('"', "")
        if len(s) > 12:
        if prop.CIMType == 101:
        t = s[4] + s[5] + '/'
        t = t + s[6] + s[7] + '/'
        t = t + s[0] + s[1] + s[2] + s[3] + " " + s[8] + s[9] + ":" + s[10] + s[11] +':' + s[12]
+ s[13]
        s = t


        return(s)
        else:
        return("")


        except:
        return("")



strComputer = "."
```

```
l = win32com.client.Dispatch("WbemScripting.SWbemLocator")
svc = l.ConnectServer(strComputer,"root\\CIMV2")
svc.Security_.AuthenticationLevel = 6
svc.Security_.ImpersonationLevel = 3
objs = svc.ExecQuery("Select * From Win32_Process")
xmldoc = win32com.client.Dispatch("MSXML2.DOMDocument")
pi = xmldoc.CreateProcessingInstruction("xml", "version='1.0' encoding='ISO-
8859-1'")
pii = xmldoc.CreateProcessingInstruction("xml-stylesheet", "type='text/xsl'
href='Process.xsl'")
xmldoc.AppendChild(pi)
xmldoc.AppendChild(pii)

oRoot = xmldoc.CreateElement("data")
for obj in objs:
oNode = xmldoc.CreateElement("Win32_Process")
for prop in obj.Properties_:
oNode1 = xmldoc.CreateElement(prop.Name)
oNode1.Text = GetValue(prop, obj)
oNode.AppendChild(oNode1)

oRoot.AppendChild(oNode)

xmldoc.AppendChild(oRoot)
ws = win32com.client.Dispatch("WScript.Shell")
xmldoc.Save(ws.CurrentDirectory + "\\Process.xml")
```

Schema XML

```
import win32com.client
import string
import sys
```

```python
reload(sys)
sys.setdefaultencoding('UTF8')
def GetValue(prop, obj):
try:
pos = 0
pos1 = 0
Name = str(prop.Name) + " = "
t = ""
s = str(obj.GetObjectText_(0))
pos = s.find(Name)
if pos > 0:
pos = pos + len(prop.Name) + 3
pos1 = len(s)
s = s[pos : pos1]
pos = s.find(";")
s = s[0 : pos]
s = s.replace("{", "")
s = s.replace("}", "")
s = s.replace('"', "")
if len(s) > 12:
if prop.CIMType == 101:
t = s[4] + s[5] + '/'
t = t + s[6] + s[7] + '/'
t = t + s[0] + s[1] + s[2] + s[3] + " " + s[8] + s[9] + ":" + s[10] + s[11] +':' + s[12] + s[13]
s = t


return(s)
else:
return("")
```

```python
    except:
        return("")


strComputer = "."
l = win32com.client.Dispatch("WbemScripting.SWbemLocator")
svc = l.ConnectServer(strComputer,"root\\CIMV2")
svc.Security_.AuthenticationLevel = 6
svc.Security_.ImpersonationLevel = 3
objs = svc.ExecQuery("Select * From Win32_Process")
xmldoc = win32com.client.Dispatch("MSXML2.DOMDocument")
pi = xmldoc.CreateProcessingInstruction("xml", "version='1.0' encoding='ISO-8859-1'")
oRoot = xmldoc.CreateElement("data")
xmldoc.AppendChild(pi)
for obj in objs:
    oNode = xmldoc.CreateElement("Win32_Process")
    for prop in obj.Properties_:
        oNode1 = xmldoc.CreateElement(prop.Name)
        oNode1.Text = GetValue(prop, obj)
        oNode.AppendChild(oNode1)

    oRoot.AppendChild(oNode)

xmldoc.AppendChild(oRoot)
ws = win32com.client.Dispatch("WScript.Shell")
xmldoc.Save(ws.CurrentDirectory + "\\ProcessE.xml")

xmldoc = None

rs = win32com.client.Dispatch("ADODB.Recordset")
```

```
rs.ActiveConnection              =               "Provider=MSDAOSP;        Data
Source=MSXML2.DSOControl;"
rs.CursorLocation = 3
rs.LockType = 3
rs.Open(ws.CurrentDirectory + "\\ProcessE.xml")
fso = win32com.client.Dispatch("Scripting.FileSystemObject")
if fso.FileExists(ws.CurrentDirectory + "\\ProcessS.xml") == True:
fso.DeleteFile(ws.CurrentDirectory + "\\ProcessS.xml")

rs.Save(ws.CurrentDirectory + "\\ProcessS.xml", 1)
```

Text Files

The many faces of Delimited Files

Text files are databases, too. You just need to know how to make them and what applications can use them to get the most from them. Below are some of the most common ones used today:

The colon delimited File

```
import win32com.client
import string
import sys

reload(sys)
sys.setdefaultencoding('UTF8')
def GetValue(prop, obj):
try:
```

```python
pos = 0
pos1 = 0
Name = str(prop.Name) + " = "
t = ""
s = str(obj.GetObjectText_(0))
pos = s.find(Name)
if pos > 0:
    pos = pos + len(prop.Name) + 3
    pos1 = len(s)
    s = s[pos : pos1]
    pos = s.find(";")
    s = s[0 : pos]
    s = s.replace("{", "")
    s = s.replace("}", "")
    s = s.replace('"', "")
    if len(s) > 12:
        if prop.CIMType == 101:
            t = s[4] + s[5] + '/'
            t = t + s[6] + s[7] + '/'
            t = t + s[0] + s[1] + s[2] + s[3] + " " + s[8] + s[9] + ":" + s[10] + s[11] +':' + s[12]
+ s[13]
            s = t


    return(s)
else:
    return("")


except:
    return("")
```

```
strComputer = "."
l = win32com.client.Dispatch("WbemScripting.SWbemLocator")
svc = l.ConnectServer(strComputer,"root\\CIMV2")
svc.Security_.AuthenticationLevel = 6
svc.Security_.ImpersonationLevel = 3
objs = svc.ExecQuery("Select * From Win32_Process")
ws = win32com.client.Dispatch("WScript.Shell")
fso = win32com.client.Dispatch("Scripting.FileSystemObject")
txtstream = fso.OpenTextFile(ws.CurrentDirectory + "\\Process.csv", 2, True, -
2)
tempstr = ""
for obj in objs:
for prop in obj.Properties_:
if tempstr != "":
tempstr = tempstr + ","

tempstr = tempstr + prop.Name

txtstream.WriteLine(tempstr)
tempstr = ""
break

tempstr = ""
for obj in objs:
for prop in obj.Properties_:
if tempstr != "":
tempstr = tempstr + ","

tempstr = tempstr + '"' + GetValue(prop, obj) + '"'
```

```
txtstream.WriteLine(tempstr)
tempstr = ""


txtstream.Close
```

The exclamation delimited File

```
import win32com.client
import string
import sys

reload(sys)
sys.setdefaultencoding('UTF8')
def GetValue(prop, obj):
try:
pos = 0
pos1 = 0
Name = str(prop.Name) + " = "
t = ""
s = str(obj.GetObjectText_(0))
pos = s.find(Name)
if pos > 0:
pos = pos + len(prop.Name) + 3
pos1 = len(s)
s = s[pos : pos1]
pos = s.find(";")
s = s[0 : pos]
```

```python
        s = s.replace("{", "")
        s = s.replace("}", "")
        s = s.replace('"', "")
        if len(s) > 12:
        if prop.CIMType == 101:
        t = s[4] + s[5] + '/'
        t = t + s[6] + s[7] + '/'
        t = t + s[0] + s[1] + s[2] + s[3] + " " + s[8] + s[9] + ":" + s[10] + s[11] +':' + s[12]
+ s[13]
        s = t


        return(s)
        else:
        return("")


        except:
        return("")



        strComputer = "."
        l = win32com.client.Dispatch("WbemScripting.SWbemLocator")
        svc = l.ConnectServer(strComputer,"root\\CIMV2")
        svc.Security_.AuthenticationLevel = 6
        svc.Security_.ImpersonationLevel = 3
        objs = svc.ExecQuery("Select * From Win32_Process")
        ws = win32com.client.Dispatch("WScript.Shell")
        fso = win32com.client.Dispatch("Scripting.FileSystemObject")
        txtstream = fso.OpenTextFile(ws.CurrentDirectory + "\\Process.txt", 2, True, -
2)
```

```
tempstr = ""
for obj in objs:
for prop in obj.Properties_:
if tempstr != "":
tempstr = tempstr + "!"

tempstr = tempstr + prop.Name

txtstream.WriteLine(tempstr)
tempstr = ""
break

tempstr = ""
for obj in objs:
for prop in obj.Properties_:
if tempstr != "":
tempstr = tempstr + "!"

tempstr = tempstr + '"' + GetValue(prop, obj) + '"'

txtstream.WriteLine(tempstr)
tempstr = ""


txtstream.Close
```

The semi-colon delimited File

```python
import win32com.client
import string
import sys

reload(sys)
sys.setdefaultencoding('UTF8')
def GetValue(prop, obj):
try:
pos = 0
pos1 = 0
Name = str(prop.Name) + " = "
t = ""
s = str(obj.GetObjectText_(0))
pos = s.find(Name)
if pos > 0:
pos = pos + len(prop.Name) + 3
pos1 = len(s)
s = s[pos : pos1]
pos = s.find(";")
s = s[0 : pos]
s = s.replace("{", "")
s = s.replace("}", "")
s = s.replace("'", "")
if len(s) > 12:
if prop.CIMType == 101:
t = s[4] + s[5] + '/'
t = t + s[6] + s[7] + '/'
t = t + s[0] + s[1] + s[2] + s[3] + " " + s[8] + s[9] + ":" + s[10] + s[11] +':' + s[12]
+ s[13]
s = t
```

```
    return(s)
else:
    return("")


except:
    return("")




strComputer = "."
l = win32com.client.Dispatch("WbemScripting.SWbemLocator")
svc = l.ConnectServer(strComputer,"root\\CIMV2")
svc.Security_.AuthenticationLevel = 6
svc.Security_.ImpersonationLevel = 3
objs = svc.ExecQuery("Select * From Win32_Process")
ws = win32com.client.Dispatch("WScript.Shell")
fso = win32com.client.Dispatch("Scripting.FileSystemObject")
txtstream = fso.OpenTextFile(ws.CurrentDirectory + "\\Process.txt", 2, True, -
2)
tempstr = ""
for obj in objs:
    for prop in obj.Properties_:
        if tempstr != "":
            tempstr = tempstr + ";"

        tempstr = tempstr + prop.Name

    txtstream.WriteLine(tempstr)
    tempstr = ""
    break
```

```
tempstr = ""
for obj in objs:
for prop in obj.Properties_:
if tempstr != "":
tempstr = tempstr + ";"

tempstr = tempstr + '"' + GetValue(prop, obj) + '"'

txtstream.WriteLine(tempstr)
tempstr = ""


txtstream.Close
```

The Tab Delimited File

```
import win32com.client
import string
import sys

reload(sys)
sys.setdefaultencoding('UTF8')
def GetValue(prop, obj):
try:
pos = 0
pos1 = 0
Name = str(prop.Name) + " = "
t = ""
s = str(obj.GetObjectText_(0))
pos = s.find(Name)
if pos > 0:
pos = pos + len(prop.Name) + 3
```

```
    pos1 = len(s)
    s = s[pos : pos1]
    pos = s.find(";")
    s = s[0 : pos]
    s = s.replace("{", "")
    s = s.replace("}", "")
    s = s.replace('"', "")
    if len(s) > 12:
    if prop.CIMType == 101:
    t = s[4] + s[5] + '/'
    t = t + s[6] + s[7] + '/'
    t = t + s[0] + s[1] + s[2] + s[3] + " " + s[8] + s[9] + ":" + s[10] + s[11] +':' + s[12]
+ s[13]
    s = t


    return(s)
    else:
    return("")


    except:
    return("")




    strComputer = "."
    l = win32com.client.Dispatch("WbemScripting.SWbemLocator")
    svc = l.ConnectServer(strComputer,"root\\CIMV2")
    svc.Security_.AuthenticationLevel = 6
    svc.Security_.ImpersonationLevel = 3
    objs = svc.ExecQuery("Select * From Win32_Process")
```

```
ws = win32com.client.Dispatch("WScript.Shell")
fso = win32com.client.Dispatch("Scripting.FileSystemObject")
txtstream = fso.OpenTextFile(ws.CurrentDirectory + "\\Process.txt", 2, True, -
```
2)
```
tempstr = ""
for obj in objs:
for prop in obj.Properties_:
if tempstr != "":
tempstr = tempstr + "\t"

tempstr = tempstr + prop.Name

txtstream.WriteLine(tempstr)
tempstr = ""
break

tempstr = ""
for obj in objs:
for prop in obj.Properties_:
if tempstr != "":
tempstr = tempstr + "\t"

tempstr = tempstr + '"' + GetValue(prop, obj) + '"'

txtstream.WriteLine(tempstr)
tempstr = ""


txtstream.Close
```

```
import win32com.client
import string
import sys

reload(sys)
sys.setdefaultencoding('UTF8')
def GetValue(prop, obj):
try:
pos = 0
pos1 = 0
Name = str(prop.Name) + " = "
t = ""
s = str(obj.GetObjectText_(0))
pos = s.find(Name)
if pos > 0:
pos = pos + len(prop.Name) + 3
pos1 = len(s)
s = s[pos : pos1]
pos = s.find(";")
s = s[0 : pos]
s = s.replace("{", "")
s = s.replace("}", "")
s = s.replace('"', "")
if len(s) > 12:
if prop.CIMType == 101:
t = s[4] + s[5] + '/'
t = t + s[6] + s[7] + '/'
t = t + s[0] + s[1] + s[2] + s[3] + " " + s[8] + s[9] + ":" + s[10] + s[11] +':' + s[12]
+ s[13]
    s = t
```

```
        return(s)
    else:
        return("")


    except:
        return("")




strComputer = "."
l = win32com.client.Dispatch("WbemScripting.SWbemLocator")
svc = l.ConnectServer(strComputer,"root\\CIMV2")
svc.Security_.AuthenticationLevel = 6
svc.Security_.ImpersonationLevel = 3
objs = svc.ExecQuery("Select * From Win32_Process")
ws = win32com.client.Dispatch("WScript.Shell")
fso = win32com.client.Dispatch("Scripting.FileSystemObject")
txtstream = fso.OpenTextFile(ws.CurrentDirectory + "\\Process.txt", 2, True, -
2)
tempstr = ""
for obj in objs:
    for prop in obj.Properties_:
        if tempstr != "":
            tempstr = tempstr + "~"

        tempstr = tempstr + prop.Name

    txtstream.WriteLine(tempstr)
    tempstr = ""
```

```
break

tempstr = ""
for obj in objs:
for prop in obj.Properties_:
if tempstr != "":
tempstr = tempstr + "~"

tempstr = tempstr + '"' + GetValue(prop, obj) + '"'

txtstream.WriteLine(tempstr)
tempstr = ""


txtstream.Close
```

Working with Excel

The Tail of three ways to do it

harbor the belief that the hardest thing a Python program should have to do is learn how to fly his or her private jet and enjoy life.

I'm not saying that the code I am providing here is going to get you there. What I am saying is the e-books that I am writing will certainly be a step in the right direction.

With that said, there are three ways to get information into excel:

CSV and Excel

```
import win32com.client
import string
import sys

reload(sys)
sys.setdefaultencoding('UTF8')
def GetValue(prop, obj):
try:
pos = 0
```

```python
        pos1 = 0
        Name = str(prop.Name) + " = "
        t = ""
        s = str(obj.GetObjectText_(0))
        pos = s.find(Name)
        if pos > 0:
        pos = pos + len(prop.Name) + 3
        pos1 = len(s)
        s = s[pos : pos1]
        pos = s.find(";")
        s = s[0 : pos]
        s = s.replace("{", "")
        s = s.replace("}", "")
        s = s.replace('"', "")
        if len(s) > 12:
        if prop.CIMType == 101:
        t = s[4] + s[5] + '/'
        t = t + s[6] + s[7] + '/'
        t = t + s[0] + s[1] + s[2] + s[3] + " " + s[8] + s[9] + ":" + s[10] + s[11] +':' + s[12] +
s[13]
        s = t


        return(s)
        else:
        return("")


        except:
        return("")



        strComputer = "."
        l = win32com.client.Dispatch("WbemScripting.SWbemLocator")
        svc = l.ConnectServer(strComputer,"root\\CIMV2")
        svc.Security_.AuthenticationLevel = 6
        svc.Security_.ImpersonationLevel = 3
        objs = svc.ExecQuery("Select * From Win32_Process")
        ws = win32com.client.Dispatch("WScript.Shell")
```

```
fso = win32com.client.Dispatch("Scripting.FileSystemObject")
txtstream = fso.OpenTextFile("D:\\Process.csv", 2, True, -2)
tempstr = ""
for obj in objs:
for prop in obj.Properties_:
if tempstr != "":
tempstr = tempstr + ","

tempstr = tempstr + prop.Name

txtstream.WriteLine(tempstr)
tempstr = ""
break

tempstr = ""
for obj in objs:
for prop in obj.Properties_:
if tempstr != "":
tempstr = tempstr + ","

tempstr = tempstr + "\"" + GetValue(prop, obj) + "\""

txtstream.WriteLine(tempstr)
tempstr = ""


txtstream.Close
txtstream = None

oExcel = win32com.client.Dispatch("Excel.Application")
oExcel.Visible = True
oExcel.Workbooks.OpenText("D:\\Process.csv")
oExcel.Columns.HorizontalAlignment = -4131
oExcel.Columns.AutoFit()
```

Excel Automation

```
import win32com.client
```

```python
import string
import sys

reload(sys)
sys.setdefaultencoding('UTF8')
def GetValue(prop, obj):
try:
pos = 0
pos1 = 0
Name = str(prop.Name) + " = "
t = ""
s = str(obj.GetObjectText_(0))
pos = s.find(Name)
if pos > 0:
pos = pos + len(prop.Name) + 3
pos1 = len(s)
s = s[pos : pos1]
pos = s.find(";")
s = s[0 : pos]
s = s.replace("{", "")
s = s.replace("}", "")
s = s.replace('"', "")
if len(s) > 12:
if prop.CIMType == 101:
t = s[4] + s[5] + '/'
t = t + s[6] + s[7] + '/'
t = t + s[0] + s[1] + s[2] + s[3] + " " + s[8] + s[9] + ":" + s[10] + s[11] +':' + s[12] +
s[13]
s = t


return(s)
else:
return("")


except:
return("")
```

```
strComputer = "."
x=1
y=2
l = win32com.client.Dispatch("WbemScripting.SWbemLocator")
svc = l.ConnectServer(strComputer,"root\\CIMV2")
svc.Security_.AuthenticationLevel = 6
svc.Security_.ImpersonationLevel = 3
objs = svc.ExecQuery("Select * From Win32_Process")
oExcel = win32com.client.Dispatch("Excel.Application")
oExcel.Visible = True
wb = oExcel.Workbooks.Add()
ws = wb.WorkSheets[0]
ws.Name = "Process"
for obj in objs:
for prop in obj.Properties_:
ws.cells(1, x).value = prop.Name
x=x+1

break

x=1
for obj in objs:
for prop in obj.Properties_:
ws.cells(y, x).value = GetValue(prop, obj)
x=x+1

x=1
y=y+1


ws.Columns.HorizontalAlignment = -4131
ws.Columns.AutoFit()
```

Excel Spreadsheet

```
import win32com.client
import string
import sys

reload(sys)
sys.setdefaultencoding('UTF8')
def GetValue(prop, obj):
try:
pos = 0
pos1 = 0
Name = str(prop.Name) + " = "
t = ""
s = str(obj.GetObjectText_(0))
pos = s.find(Name)
if pos > 0:
pos = pos + len(prop.Name) + 3
pos1 = len(s)
s = s[pos : pos1]
pos = s.find(";")
s = s[0 : pos]
s = s.replace("{", "")
s = s.replace("}", "")
s = s.replace('"', "")
if len(s) > 12:
if prop.CIMType == 101:
t = s[4] + s[5] + '/'
t = t + s[6] + s[7] + '/'
t = t + s[0] + s[1] + s[2] + s[3] + " " + s[8] + s[9] + ":" + s[10] + s[11] +':' + s[12] +
s[13]
s = t


return(s)
else:
return("")
```

```
    except:
      return("")




    strComputer = "."
    l = win32com.client.Dispatch("WbemScripting.SWbemLocator")
    svc = l.ConnectServer(strComputer,"root\\CIMV2")
    svc.Security_.AuthenticationLevel = 6
    svc.Security_.ImpersonationLevel = 3
    objs = svc.ExecQuery("Select * From Win32_Process")
    ws = win32com.client.Dispatch("WScript.Shell")
    fso = win32com.client.Dispatch("Scripting.FileSystemObject")
    txtstream = fso.OpenTextFile(ws.CurrentDirectory + "\\ProcessExcel.xml", 2,
True, -2)
    txtstream.WriteLine("<?xml version='1.0'?>")
    txtstream.WriteLine("<?mso-application progid='Excel.Sheet'?>")
    txtstream.WriteLine("<Workbook          xmlns='urn:schemas-microsoft-
com:office:spreadsheet'        xmlns:o='urn:schemas-microsoft-com:office:office'
xmlns:x='urn:schemas-microsoft-com:office:excel'        xmlns:ss='urn:schemas-
microsoft-com:office:spreadsheet'        xmlns:html='http://www.w3.org/TR/REC-
html40'>")
    txtstream.WriteLine(" <DocumentProperties    xmlns='urn:schemas-microsoft-
com:office:office'>")
    txtstream.WriteLine("          <Author>Windows User</Author>")
    txtstream.WriteLine("          <LastAuthor>Windows User</LastAuthor>")
    txtstream.WriteLine("          <Created>2007-11-27T19:36:16Z</Created>")
    txtstream.WriteLine("          <Version>12.00</Version>")
    txtstream.WriteLine(" </DocumentProperties>")
    txtstream.WriteLine(" <ExcelWorkbook          xmlns='urn:schemas-microsoft-
com:office:excel'>")
    txtstream.WriteLine("          <WindowHeight>11835</WindowHeight>")
    txtstream.WriteLine("          <WindowWidth>18960</WindowWidth>")
    txtstream.WriteLine("          <WindowTopX>120</WindowTopX>")
    txtstream.WriteLine("          <WindowTopY>135</WindowTopY>")
    txtstream.WriteLine("          <ProtectStructure>False</ProtectStructure>")
    txtstream.WriteLine("          <ProtectWindows>False</ProtectWindows>")
    txtstream.WriteLine(" </ExcelWorkbook>")
    txtstream.WriteLine(" <Styles>")
```

```
txtstream.WriteLine("                    <Style ss:ID='Default' ss:Name='Normal'>")
txtstream.WriteLine("                        <Alignment ss:Vertical='Bottom'/>")
txtstream.WriteLine("                        <Borders/>")
txtstream.WriteLine("                        <Font            ss:FontName='Calibri'
x:Family='Swiss' ss:Size='11' ss:Color='#000000'/>")
txtstream.WriteLine("                        <Interior/>")
txtstream.WriteLine("                        <NumberFormat/>")
txtstream.WriteLine("                        <Protection/>")
txtstream.WriteLine("                </Style>")
txtstream.WriteLine("                <Style ss:ID='s62'>")
txtstream.WriteLine("                        <Borders/>")
txtstream.WriteLine("                        <Font            ss:FontName='Calibri'
x:Family='Swiss' ss:Size='11' ss:Color='#000000' ss:Bold='1'/>")
txtstream.WriteLine("                </Style>")
txtstream.WriteLine("                <Style ss:ID='s63'>")
txtstream.WriteLine("                        <Alignment        ss:Horizontal='Left'
ss:Vertical='Bottom' ss:Indent='2'/>")
txtstream.WriteLine("                        <Font        ss:FontName='Verdana'
x:Family='Swiss' ss:Size='7.7' ss:Color='#000000'/>")
txtstream.WriteLine("                </Style>")
txtstream.WriteLine("    </Styles>")

txtstream.WriteLine("<Worksheet ss:Name='Process'>")
txtstream.WriteLine("                <Table      x:FullColumns='1'      x:FullRows='1'
ss:DefaultRowHeight='24.9375'>")
txtstream.WriteLine("                <Column  ss:AutoFitWidth='1'  ss:Width='82.5'
ss:Span='5'/>")
for obj in objs:
txtstream.WriteLine("     <Row ss:AutoFitHeight='0'>")
for prop in obj.Properties_:
txtstream.WriteLine("            <Cell ss:StyleID='s62'><Data ss:Type='String'>" +
prop.Name + "</Data></Cell>")

txtstream.WriteLine("        </Row>")
break


for obj in objs:
txtstream.WriteLine("     <Row ss:AutoFitHeight='0' ss:Height='13.5'>")
for prop in obj.Properties_:
```

```
txtstream.WriteLine("                        <Cell><Data ss:Type='String'><![CDATA[" +
GetValue(prop, obj) + "]]></Data></Cell>")

txtstream.WriteLine("     </Row>")


txtstream.WriteLine("  </Table>")
txtstream.WriteLine(" <WorksheetOptions        xmlns='urn:schemas-microsoft-
com:office:excel'>")
txtstream.WriteLine("             <PageSetup>")
txtstream.WriteLine("                  <Header x:Margin='0.3'/>")
txtstream.WriteLine("                  <Footer x:Margin='0.3'/>")
txtstream.WriteLine("                  <PageMargins          x:Bottom='0.75'
x:Left='0.7' x:Right='0.7' x:Top='0.75'/>")
txtstream.WriteLine("             </PageSetup>")
txtstream.WriteLine("             <Unsynced/>")
txtstream.WriteLine("            <Print>")
txtstream.WriteLine("                   <FitHeight>0</FitHeight>")
txtstream.WriteLine("                   <ValidPrinterInfo/>")
txtstream.WriteLine("
     <HorizontalResolution>600</HorizontalResolution>")
txtstream.WriteLine("
     <VerticalResolution>600</VerticalResolution>")
txtstream.WriteLine("             </Print>")
txtstream.WriteLine("            <Selected/>")
txtstream.WriteLine("            <Panes>")
txtstream.WriteLine("                   <Pane>")
txtstream.WriteLine("                            <Number>3</Number>")
txtstream.WriteLine("                            <ActiveRow>9</ActiveRow>")
txtstream.WriteLine("                            <ActiveCol>7</ActiveCol>")
txtstream.WriteLine("                   </Pane>")
txtstream.WriteLine("            </Panes>")
txtstream.WriteLine("            <ProtectObjects>False</ProtectObjects>")
txtstream.WriteLine("            <ProtectScenarios>False</ProtectScenarios>")
txtstream.WriteLine(" </WorksheetOptions>")
txtstream.WriteLine("</Worksheet>")
txtstream.WriteLine("</Workbook>")
txtstream.Close()
ws.Run(ws.CurrentDirectory + "\\ProcessExcel.xml")
```

Python WMI and XSL
Rendering your XML Files in Style

Nothing is prettier than a quality XSL stylesheet.
—R. T. Edwards

There is nothing great about xml when you're just looking at an xml file. But as soon as you add an HTML based XSL file to render it, suddenly, it looks professional and understandable.

There four ways to use xsl, Single Line Horizontal, Multi line Horizontal, Single Line Vertical and Multi line Vertical.

Single Line Horizontal Example

```
import win32com.client
import string
import sys

reload(sys)
sys.setdefaultencoding('UTF8')
def GetValue(prop, obj):
    try:
        pos = 0
        pos1 = 0
```

```python
        Name = str(prop.Name) + " = "
        t = ""
        s = str(obj.GetObjectText_(0))
        pos = s.find(Name)
        if pos > 0:
            pos = pos + len(prop.Name) + 3
            pos1 = len(s)
            s = s[pos : pos1]
            pos = s.find(";")
            s = s[0 : pos]
            s = s.replace("{", "")
            s = s.replace("}", "")
            s = s.replace('"', "")
            if len(s) > 12:
                if prop.CIMType == 101:
                    t = s[4] + s[5] + '/'
                    t = t + s[6] + s[7] + '/'
                    t = t + s[0] + s[1] + s[2] + s[3] + " " + s[8] + s[9] + ":" + s[10] + s[11]
+':' + s[12] + s[13]
                    s = t


        return(s)
      else:
        return("")

    except:
        return("")




strComputer = "."
l = win32com.client.Dispatch("WbemScripting.SWbemLocator")
svc = l.ConnectServer(strComputer,"root\\CIMV2")
svc.Security_.AuthenticationLevel = 6
svc.Security_.ImpersonationLevel = 3
objs = svc.ExecQuery("Select * From Win32_Process")
ws = win32com.client.Dispatch("WScript.Shell")
fso = win32com.client.Dispatch("Scripting.FileSystemObject")
```

```
txtstream= fso.OpenTextfile(ws.CurrentDirectory + "\\Process.xsl", 2, True, -2)
txtstream.WriteLine("<?xml version='1.0' encoding='iso-8859-1'?>")
txtstream.WriteLine("<xsl:stylesheet                                   version=\"1.0\"
xmlns:xsl=\"http://www.w3.org/1999/XSL/Transform\">")
txtstream.WriteLine("<xsl:template match=\"/\">")
txtstream.WriteLine("<html>")
txtstream.WriteLine("<head>")
txtstream.WriteLine("<title>Process</title>")
txtstream.WriteLine("<style type='text/css'>")
txtstream.WriteLine("th")
txtstream.WriteLine("{")
txtstream.WriteLine("    COLOR: white;")
txtstream.WriteLine("    BACKGROUND-COLOR: navy;")
txtstream.WriteLine("    FONT-FAMILY: Cambria, serif;")
txtstream.WriteLine("    FONT-SIZE: 12px;")
txtstream.WriteLine("    text-align: left;")
txtstream.WriteLine("    white-Space: nowrap;")
txtstream.WriteLine("}")
txtstream.WriteLine("td")
txtstream.WriteLine("{")
txtstream.WriteLine("    COLOR: navy;")
txtstream.WriteLine("    FONT-FAMILY: Cambria, serif;")
txtstream.WriteLine("    FONT-SIZE: 12px;")
txtstream.WriteLine("    text-align: left;")
txtstream.WriteLine("    white-Space: nowrap;")
txtstream.WriteLine("}")
txtstream.WriteLine("div")
txtstream.WriteLine("{")
txtstream.WriteLine("    COLOR: navy;")
txtstream.WriteLine("    FONT-FAMILY: Cambria, serif;")
txtstream.WriteLine("    FONT-SIZE: 12px;")
txtstream.WriteLine("    text-align: left;")
txtstream.WriteLine("    white-Space: nowrap;")
txtstream.WriteLine("}")
txtstream.WriteLine("span")
txtstream.WriteLine("{")
txtstream.WriteLine("    COLOR: navy;")
txtstream.WriteLine("    FONT-FAMILY: Cambria, serif;")
txtstream.WriteLine("    FONT-SIZE: 12px;")
txtstream.WriteLine("    text-align: left;")
```

83

```
txtstream.WriteLine("    white-Space: nowrap;")
txtstream.WriteLine("    width: 100%;")
txtstream.WriteLine("}")
txtstream.WriteLine("textarea")
txtstream.WriteLine("{")
txtstream.WriteLine("    COLOR: navy;")
txtstream.WriteLine("    FONT-FAMILY: Cambria, serif;")
txtstream.WriteLine("    FONT-SIZE: 12px;")
txtstream.WriteLine("    text-align: left;")
txtstream.WriteLine("    white-Space: nowrap;")
txtstream.WriteLine("    display:inline-block;")
txtstream.WriteLine("    width: 100%;")
txtstream.WriteLine("}")
txtstream.WriteLine("select")
txtstream.WriteLine("{")
txtstream.WriteLine("    COLOR: navy;")
txtstream.WriteLine("    FONT-FAMILY: Cambria, serif;")
txtstream.WriteLine("    FONT-SIZE: 10px;")
txtstream.WriteLine("    text-align: left;")
txtstream.WriteLine("    white-Space: nowrap;")
txtstream.WriteLine("    display:inline-block;")
txtstream.WriteLine("    width: 100%;")
txtstream.WriteLine("}")
txtstream.WriteLine("input")
txtstream.WriteLine("{")
txtstream.WriteLine("    COLOR: navy;")
txtstream.WriteLine("    FONT-FAMILY: Cambria, serif;")
txtstream.WriteLine("    FONT-SIZE: 12px;")
txtstream.WriteLine("    text-align: left;")
txtstream.WriteLine("    display:table-cell;")
txtstream.WriteLine("    white-Space: nowrap;")
txtstream.WriteLine("}")
txtstream.WriteLine("h1 {")
txtstream.WriteLine("color: antiquewhite;")
txtstream.WriteLine("text-shadow: 1px 1px 1px black;")
txtstream.WriteLine("padding: 3px;")
txtstream.WriteLine("text-align: center;")
txtstream.WriteLine("box-shadow: invar 2px 2px 5px rgba(0,0,0,0.5), invar -2px
-2px 5px rgba(255,255,255,0.5)")
txtstream.WriteLine("}")
```

```
txtstream.WriteLine("tr:nth-child(even){background-color:#f2f2f2;}")
txtstream.WriteLine("tr:nth-child(odd){background-color:#cccccc;
color:#f2f2f2;}")
txtstream.WriteLine("</style>")
txtstream.WriteLine("</head>")
txtstream.WriteLine("<body>")
txtstream.WriteLine("<table Width ='100%'>")
for obj in objs:
    txtstream.writeline("<tr>")
    for prop in obj.Properties_:
        txtstream.writeline("<th  align='left'  nowrap='true'>" + prop.Name +
"</th>")

    txtstream.writeline("</tr>")
    break

for obj in objs:
    txtstream.writeline("<tr>")
    for prop in obj.Properties_:
        txtstream.writeline("<td       align='left'      nowrap='true'><xsl:value-of
select=\"data/Win32_Process/" + prop.Name + "\"/></td>")

    txtstream.writeline("</tr>")
    break

txtstream.WriteLine("</table>")
txtstream.WriteLine("</body>")
txtstream.WriteLine("</html>")
txtstream.WriteLine("</xsl:template>")
txtstream.WriteLine("</xsl:stylesheet>")
txtstream.Close()
```

```
import win32com.client
import string
import sys

reload(sys)
sys.setdefaultencoding('UTF8')
def GetValue(prop, obj):
   try:
     pos = 0
     pos1 = 0
     Name = str(prop.Name) + " = "
     t = ""
     s = str(obj.GetObjectText_(0))
     pos = s.find(Name)
     if pos > 0:
        pos = pos + len(prop.Name) + 3
        pos1 = len(s)
        s = s[pos : pos1]
        pos = s.find(";")
        s = s[0 : pos]
        s = s.replace("{", "")
        s = s.replace("}", "")
        s = s.replace('"', "")
        if len(s) > 12:
           if prop.CIMType == 101:
              t = s[4] + s[5] + '/'
              t = t + s[6] + s[7] + '/'
              t = t + s[0] + s[1] + s[2] + s[3] + " " + s[8] + s[9] + ":" + s[10] + s[11]
+':' + s[12] + s[13]
              s = t


        return(s)
     else:
        return("")
```

```
    except:
        return("")




    strComputer = "."
    l = win32com.client.Dispatch("WbemScripting.SWbemLocator")
    svc = l.ConnectServer(strComputer,"root\\CIMV2")
    svc.Security_.AuthenticationLevel = 6
    svc.Security_.ImpersonationLevel = 3
    objs = svc.ExecQuery("Select * From Win32_Process")
    ws = win32com.client.Dispatch("WScript.Shell")
    fso = win32com.client.Dispatch("Scripting.FileSystemObject")
    txtstream= fso.OpenTextfile(ws.CurrentDirectory + "\\Process.xsl", 2, True, -2)
    txtstream.WriteLine("<?xml version='1.0' encoding='iso-8859-1'?>")
    txtstream.WriteLine("<xsl:stylesheet                version=\"1.0\"
xmlns:xsl=\"http://www.w3.org/1999/XSL/Transform\">")
    txtstream.WriteLine("<xsl:template match=\"/\">")
    txtstream.WriteLine("<html>")
    txtstream.WriteLine("<head>")
    txtstream.WriteLine("<title>Process</title>")
    txtstream.WriteLine("<style type='text/css'>")
    txtstream.WriteLine("th")
    txtstream.WriteLine("{")
    txtstream.WriteLine("   COLOR: white;")
    txtstream.WriteLine("   BACKGROUND-COLOR: navy;")
    txtstream.WriteLine("   FONT-FAMILY: Cambria, serif;")
    txtstream.WriteLine("   FONT-SIZE: 12px;")
    txtstream.WriteLine("   text-align: left;")
    txtstream.WriteLine("   white-Space: nowrap;")
    txtstream.WriteLine("}")
    txtstream.WriteLine("td")
    txtstream.WriteLine("{")
    txtstream.WriteLine("   COLOR: navy;")
    txtstream.WriteLine("   FONT-FAMILY: Cambria, serif;")
    txtstream.WriteLine("   FONT-SIZE: 12px;")
    txtstream.WriteLine("   text-align: left;")
    txtstream.WriteLine("   white-Space: nowrap;")
    txtstream.WriteLine("}")
```

```
txtstream.WriteLine("div")
txtstream.WriteLine("{")
txtstream.WriteLine("    COLOR: navy;")
txtstream.WriteLine("    FONT-FAMILY: Cambria, serif;")
txtstream.WriteLine("    FONT-SIZE: 12px;")
txtstream.WriteLine("    text-align: left;")
txtstream.WriteLine("    white-Space: nowrap;")
txtstream.WriteLine("}")
txtstream.WriteLine("span")
txtstream.WriteLine("{")
txtstream.WriteLine("    COLOR: navy;")
txtstream.WriteLine("    FONT-FAMILY: Cambria, serif;")
txtstream.WriteLine("    FONT-SIZE: 12px;")
txtstream.WriteLine("    text-align: left;")
txtstream.WriteLine("    white-Space: nowrap;")
txtstream.WriteLine("    width: 100%;")
txtstream.WriteLine("}")
txtstream.WriteLine("textarea")
txtstream.WriteLine("{")
txtstream.WriteLine("    COLOR: navy;")
txtstream.WriteLine("    FONT-FAMILY: Cambria, serif;")
txtstream.WriteLine("    FONT-SIZE: 12px;")
txtstream.WriteLine("    text-align: left;")
txtstream.WriteLine("    white-Space: nowrap;")
txtstream.WriteLine("    display:inline-block;")
txtstream.WriteLine("    width: 100%;")
txtstream.WriteLine("}")
txtstream.WriteLine("select")
txtstream.WriteLine("{")
txtstream.WriteLine("    COLOR: navy;")
txtstream.WriteLine("    FONT-FAMILY: Cambria, serif;")
txtstream.WriteLine("    FONT-SIZE: 10px;")
txtstream.WriteLine("    text-align: left;")
txtstream.WriteLine("    white-Space: nowrap;")
txtstream.WriteLine("    display:inline-block;")
txtstream.WriteLine("    width: 100%;")
txtstream.WriteLine("}")
txtstream.WriteLine("input")
txtstream.WriteLine("{")
txtstream.WriteLine("    COLOR: navy;")
```

```
txtstream.WriteLine("    FONT-FAMILY: Cambria, serif;")
txtstream.WriteLine("    FONT-SIZE: 12px;")
txtstream.WriteLine("    text-align: left;")
txtstream.WriteLine("    display:table-cell;")
txtstream.WriteLine("    white-Space: nowrap;")
txtstream.WriteLine("}")
txtstream.WriteLine("h1 {")
txtstream.WriteLine("color: antiquewhite;")
txtstream.WriteLine("text-shadow: 1px 1px 1px black;")
txtstream.WriteLine("padding: 3px;")
txtstream.WriteLine("text-align: center;")
txtstream.WriteLine("box-shadow: invar 2px 2px 5px rgba(0,0,0,0.5), invar -2px
-2px 5px rgba(255,255,255,0.5)")
txtstream.WriteLine("}")
txtstream.WriteLine("tr:nth-child(even){background-color:#f2f2f2;}")
txtstream.WriteLine("tr:nth-child(odd){background-color:#cccccc;
color:#f2f2f2;}")
txtstream.WriteLine("</style>")
txtstream.WriteLine("</head>")
txtstream.WriteLine("<body>")
txtstream.WriteLine("<table Width ='100%'>")
for obj in objs:
    txtstream.writeline("<tr>")
    for prop in obj.Properties_:
        txtstream.writeline("<th  align='left'  nowrap='true'>" + prop.Name +
"</th>")

    txtstream.writeline("</tr>")
    break

for obj in objs:
    txtstream.writeline("<xsl:for-each select=\"data\Win32_Process\">")
    txtstream.writeline("<tr>")
    for prop in obj.Properties_:
        txtstream.writeline("<td       align='left'       nowrap='true'><xsl:value-of
select=\"" + prop.Name + "\"/></td>")

    txtstream.writeline("</tr>")
    txtstream.writeline("</xsl:for-each>")
    break
```

```
txtstream.WriteLine("</table>")
txtstream.WriteLine("</body>")
txtstream.WriteLine("</html>")
txtstream.WriteLine("</xsl:template>")
txtstream.WriteLine("</xsl:stylesheet>")
txtstream.Close()
```

Single Line Vertical

```
import win32com.client
import string
import sys

reload(sys)
sys.setdefaultencoding('UTF8')
def GetValue(prop, obj):
   try:
     pos = 0
     pos1 = 0
     Name = str(prop.Name) + " = "
     t = ""
     s = str(obj.GetObjectText_(0))
     pos = s.find(Name)
     if pos > 0:
        pos = pos + len(prop.Name) + 3
        pos1 = len(s)
        s = s[pos : pos1]
        pos = s.find(";")
        s = s[0 : pos]
        s = s.replace("{", "")
        s = s.replace("}", "")
        s = s.replace('"', "")
        if len(s) > 12:
           if prop.CIMType == 101:
              t = s[4] + s[5] + '/'
              t = t + s[6] + s[7] + '/'
```

```
            t = t + s[0] + s[1] + s[2] + s[3] + " " + s[8] + s[9] + ":" + s[10] + s[11]
+':' + s[12] + s[13]
            s = t


        return(s)
      else:
        return("")


    except:
      return("")




    strComputer = "."
    l = win32com.client.Dispatch("WbemScripting.SWbemLocator")
    svc = l.ConnectServer(strComputer,"root\\CIMV2")
    svc.Security_.AuthenticationLevel = 6
    svc.Security_.ImpersonationLevel = 3
    objs = svc.ExecQuery("Select * From Win32_Process")
    ws = win32com.client.Dispatch("WScript.Shell")
    fso = win32com.client.Dispatch("Scripting.FileSystemObject")
    txtstream= fso.OpenTextfile(ws.CurrentDirectory + "\\Process.xsl", 2, True, -2)
    txtstream.WriteLine("<?xml version='1.0' encoding='iso-8859-1'?>")
    txtstream.WriteLine("<xsl:stylesheet                          version=\"1.0\"
xmlns:xsl=\"http://www.w3.org/1999/XSL/Transform\">")
    txtstream.WriteLine("<xsl:template match=\"/\">")
    txtstream.WriteLine("<html>")
    txtstream.WriteLine("<head>")
    txtstream.WriteLine("<title>Process</title>")
    txtstream.WriteLine("<style type='text/css'>")
    txtstream.WriteLine("th")
    txtstream.WriteLine("{")
    txtstream.WriteLine("    COLOR: white;")
    txtstream.WriteLine("    BACKGROUND-COLOR: navy;")
    txtstream.WriteLine("    FONT-FAMILY: Cambria, serif;")
    txtstream.WriteLine("    FONT-SIZE: 12px;")
    txtstream.WriteLine("    text-align: left;")
    txtstream.WriteLine("    white-Space: nowrap;")
```

```
txtstream.WriteLine("}")
txtstream.WriteLine("td")
txtstream.WriteLine("{")
txtstream.WriteLine("    COLOR: navy;")
txtstream.WriteLine("    FONT-FAMILY: Cambria, serif;")
txtstream.WriteLine("    FONT-SIZE: 12px;")
txtstream.WriteLine("    text-align: left;")
txtstream.WriteLine("    white-Space: nowrap;")
txtstream.WriteLine("}")
txtstream.WriteLine("div")
txtstream.WriteLine("{")
txtstream.WriteLine("    COLOR: navy;")
txtstream.WriteLine("    FONT-FAMILY: Cambria, serif;")
txtstream.WriteLine("    FONT-SIZE: 12px;")
txtstream.WriteLine("    text-align: left;")
txtstream.WriteLine("    white-Space: nowrap;")
txtstream.WriteLine("}")
txtstream.WriteLine("span")
txtstream.WriteLine("{")
txtstream.WriteLine("    COLOR: navy;")
txtstream.WriteLine("    FONT-FAMILY: Cambria, serif;")
txtstream.WriteLine("    FONT-SIZE: 12px;")
txtstream.WriteLine("    text-align: left;")
txtstream.WriteLine("    white-Space: nowrap;")
txtstream.WriteLine("    width: 100%;")
txtstream.WriteLine("}")
txtstream.WriteLine("textarea")
txtstream.WriteLine("{")
txtstream.WriteLine("    COLOR: navy;")
txtstream.WriteLine("    FONT-FAMILY: Cambria, serif;")
txtstream.WriteLine("    FONT-SIZE: 12px;")
txtstream.WriteLine("    text-align: left;")
txtstream.WriteLine("    white-Space: nowrap;")
txtstream.WriteLine("    display:inline-block;")
txtstream.WriteLine("    width: 100%;")
txtstream.WriteLine("}")
txtstream.WriteLine("select")
txtstream.WriteLine("{")
txtstream.WriteLine("    COLOR: navy;")
txtstream.WriteLine("    FONT-FAMILY: Cambria, serif;")
```

```
txtstream.WriteLine("   FONT-SIZE: 10px;")
txtstream.WriteLine("   text-align: left;")
txtstream.WriteLine("   white-Space: nowrap;")
txtstream.WriteLine("   display:inline-block;")
txtstream.WriteLine("   width: 100%;")
txtstream.WriteLine("}")
txtstream.WriteLine("input")
txtstream.WriteLine("{")
txtstream.WriteLine("   COLOR: navy;")
txtstream.WriteLine("   FONT-FAMILY: Cambria, serif;")
txtstream.WriteLine("   FONT-SIZE: 12px;")
txtstream.WriteLine("   text-align: left;")
txtstream.WriteLine("   display:table-cell;")
txtstream.WriteLine("   white-Space: nowrap;")
txtstream.WriteLine("}")
txtstream.WriteLine("h1 {")
txtstream.WriteLine("color: antiquewhite;")
txtstream.WriteLine("text-shadow: 1px 1px 1px black;")
txtstream.WriteLine("padding: 3px;")
txtstream.WriteLine("text-align: center;")
txtstream.WriteLine("box-shadow: invar 2px 2px 5px rgba(0,0,0,0.5), invar -2px
-2px 5px rgba(255,255,255,0.5))")
txtstream.WriteLine("}")
txtstream.WriteLine("tr:nth-child(even){background-color:#f2f2f2;}")
txtstream.WriteLine("tr:nth-child(odd){background-color:#cccccc;
color:#f2f2f2;}")
txtstream.WriteLine("</style>")
txtstream.WriteLine("</head>")
txtstream.WriteLine("<body>")
txtstream.WriteLine("<table Width ='100%'>")
for obj in objs:

    for prop in obj.Properties_:
        txtstream.writeline("<tr><th align='left' nowrap='true'>" + prop.Name +
"</th><td align='left' nowrap='true'><xsl:value-of select=\"data/Win32_Process/"
+ prop.Name + "\"/></td></tr>")

    txtstream.writeline("</tr>")
    break
```

```
txtstream.WriteLine("</table>")
txtstream.WriteLine("</body>")
txtstream.WriteLine("</html>")
txtstream.WriteLine("</xsl:template>")
txtstream.WriteLine("</xsl:stylesheet>")
txtstream.Close()
```

Multi Line Vertical

```
import win32com.client
import string
import sys

reload(sys)
sys.setdefaultencoding('UTF8')
def GetValue(prop, obj):
  try:
    pos = 0
    pos1 = 0
    Name = str(prop.Name) + " = "
    t = ""
    s = str(obj.GetObjectText_(0))
    pos = s.find(Name)
    if pos > 0:
      pos = pos + len(prop.Name) + 3
      pos1 = len(s)
      s = s[pos : pos1]
      pos = s.find(";")
      s = s[0 : pos]
      s = s.replace("{", "")
      s = s.replace("}", "")
      s = s.replace('"', "")
      if len(s) > 12:
        if prop.CIMType == 101:
          t = s[4] + s[5] + '/'
          t = t + s[6] + s[7] + '/'
```

```
        t = t + s[0] + s[1] + s[2] + s[3] + " " + s[8] + s[9] + ":" + s[10] + s[11] +':' +
s[12] + s[13]
          s = t


     return(s)
   else:
     return("")

 except:
   return("")



strComputer = "."
l = win32com.client.Dispatch("WbemScripting.SWbemLocator")
svc = l.ConnectServer(strComputer,"root\\CIMV2")
svc.Security_.AuthenticationLevel = 6
svc.Security_.ImpersonationLevel = 3
objs = svc.ExecQuery("Select * From Win32_Process")
ws = win32com.client.Dispatch("WScript.Shell")
fso = win32com.client.Dispatch("Scripting.FileSystemObject")
txtstream= fso.OpenTextfile(ws.CurrentDirectory + "\\Process.xsl", 2, True, -2)
txtstream.WriteLine("<?xml version='1.0' encoding='iso-8859-1'?>")
txtstream.WriteLine("<xsl:stylesheet                          version=\"1.0\"
xmlns:xsl=\"http://www.w3.org/1999/XSL/Transform\">")
txtstream.WriteLine("<xsl:template match=\"/\">")
txtstream.WriteLine("<html>")
txtstream.WriteLine("<head>")
txtstream.WriteLine("<title>Process</title>")
txtstream.WriteLine("<style type='text/css'>")
txtstream.WriteLine("th")
txtstream.WriteLine("{")
txtstream.WriteLine("   COLOR: white;")
txtstream.WriteLine("   BACKGROUND-COLOR: navy;")
txtstream.WriteLine("   FONT-FAMILY: Cambria, serif;")
txtstream.WriteLine("   FONT-SIZE: 12px;")
txtstream.WriteLine("   text-align: left;")
txtstream.WriteLine("   white-Space: nowrap;")
```

```
txtstream.WriteLine("}")
txtstream.WriteLine("td")
txtstream.WriteLine("{")
txtstream.WriteLine("    COLOR: navy;")
txtstream.WriteLine("    FONT-FAMILY: Cambria, serif;")
txtstream.WriteLine("    FONT-SIZE: 12px;")
txtstream.WriteLine("    text-align: left;")
txtstream.WriteLine("    white-Space: nowrap;")
txtstream.WriteLine("}")
txtstream.WriteLine("div")
txtstream.WriteLine("{")
txtstream.WriteLine("    COLOR: navy;")
txtstream.WriteLine("    FONT-FAMILY: Cambria, serif;")
txtstream.WriteLine("    FONT-SIZE: 12px;")
txtstream.WriteLine("    text-align: left;")
txtstream.WriteLine("    white-Space: nowrap;")
txtstream.WriteLine("}")
txtstream.WriteLine("span")
txtstream.WriteLine("{")
txtstream.WriteLine("    COLOR: navy;")
txtstream.WriteLine("    FONT-FAMILY: Cambria, serif;")
txtstream.WriteLine("    FONT-SIZE: 12px;")
txtstream.WriteLine("    text-align: left;")
txtstream.WriteLine("    white-Space: nowrap;")
txtstream.WriteLine("    width: 100%;")
txtstream.WriteLine("}")
txtstream.WriteLine("textarea")
txtstream.WriteLine("{")
txtstream.WriteLine("    COLOR: navy;")
txtstream.WriteLine("    FONT-FAMILY: Cambria, serif;")
txtstream.WriteLine("    FONT-SIZE: 12px;")
txtstream.WriteLine("    text-align: left;")
txtstream.WriteLine("    white-Space: nowrap;")
txtstream.WriteLine("    display:inline-block;")
txtstream.WriteLine("    width: 100%;")
txtstream.WriteLine("}")
txtstream.WriteLine("select")
txtstream.WriteLine("{")
txtstream.WriteLine("    COLOR: navy;")
txtstream.WriteLine("    FONT-FAMILY: Cambria, serif;")
```

```
txtstream.WriteLine("    FONT-SIZE: 10px;")
txtstream.WriteLine("    text-align: left;")
txtstream.WriteLine("    white-Space: nowrap;")
txtstream.WriteLine("    display:inline-block;")
txtstream.WriteLine("    width: 100%;")
txtstream.WriteLine("}")
txtstream.WriteLine("input")
txtstream.WriteLine("{")
txtstream.WriteLine("    COLOR: navy;")
txtstream.WriteLine("    FONT-FAMILY: Cambria, serif;")
txtstream.WriteLine("    FONT-SIZE: 12px;")
txtstream.WriteLine("    text-align: left;")
txtstream.WriteLine("    display:table-cell;")
txtstream.WriteLine("    white-Space: nowrap;")
txtstream.WriteLine("}")
txtstream.WriteLine("h1 {")
txtstream.WriteLine("color: antiquewhite;")
txtstream.WriteLine("text-shadow: 1px 1px 1px black;")
txtstream.WriteLine("padding: 3px;")
txtstream.WriteLine("text-align: center;")
txtstream.WriteLine("box-shadow: invar 2px 2px 5px rgba(0,0,0,0.5), invar -2px -
2px 5px rgba(255,255,255,0.5)")
txtstream.WriteLine("}")
txtstream.WriteLine("tr:nth-child(even){background-color:#f2f2f2;}")
txtstream.WriteLine("tr:nth-child(odd){background-color:#cccccc; color:#f2f2f2;}")
txtstream.WriteLine("</style>")
txtstream.WriteLine("</head>")
txtstream.WriteLine("<body>")
txtstream.WriteLine("<table Width ='100%'>")
for obj in objs:
    for prop in obj.Properties_:
        txtstream.writeline("<tr><th  align='left'  nowrap='true'>" + prop.Name +
"</th><xsl:for-each         select=\"data\Win32_Process\"><td         align='left'
nowrap='true'><xsl:value-of   select=\""   +   prop.Name   +   "\"/></td></xsl:for-
each></tr>")

    break

txtstream.WriteLine("</table>")
txtstream.WriteLine("</body>")
```

```
txtstream.WriteLine("</html>")
txtstream.WriteLine("</xsl:template>")
txtstream.WriteLine("</xsl:stylesheet>")
txtstream.Close()
```

Python WMI and HTA

The difference between HTML and HTA

There's nothing wrong with trying something new
when you know something new is worth your time
and effort.
—R. T. Edwards

Thedifference between HTA and HTML is HTA gives you a older browser to work with and you have a standalone visual interface that works like an exe. Below, is an example on what the code looks like and what the output looks like when you run it.

Stylesheets
Do you proud every time

Stylesheets aren't just to make a page look remarkable, they also make you look remarkable, too.
— R. T. Edwards

What is the first thing you see when you go to a website and look at the home page for the first time? It is the level of professionalism – that keen insight to attention to details – that draws you in. Speaks to you. Tells you that the site wants you to stay a while and shares with you a common ground.

The unseen hero – css. I've created some stylesheets—listed below—so you can try and use with the various web related programs.

NONE

```
txtstream.WriteLine("<style type='text/css'>")
txtstream.WriteLine("th")
txtstream.WriteLine("")
txtstream.WriteLine("   COLOR: white;")
txtstream.WriteLine(" Next")
txtstream.WriteLine("td")
txtstream.WriteLine("")
```

```
txtstream.WriteLine("    COLOR: white;")
txtstream.WriteLine(" Next")
txtstream.WriteLine("</style>")
```

BLACK AND WHITE TEXT

```
txtstream.WriteLine("<style type='text/css'>")
txtstream.WriteLine("th")
txtstream.WriteLine("")
txtstream.WriteLine("    COLOR: white;")
txtstream.WriteLine("    BACKGROUND-COLOR: black;")
txtstream.WriteLine("    FONT-FAMILY: Cambria, serif;")
txtstream.WriteLine("    FONT-SIZE: 12px;")
txtstream.WriteLine("    text-align: left;")
txtstream.WriteLine("    white-Space: nowrap;")
txtstream.WriteLine(" Next")
txtstream.WriteLine("td")
txtstream.WriteLine("")
txtstream.WriteLine("    COLOR: white;")
txtstream.WriteLine("    BACKGROUND-COLOR: black;")
txtstream.WriteLine("    FONT-FAMILY: Cambria, serif;")
txtstream.WriteLine("    FONT-SIZE: 12px;")
txtstream.WriteLine("    text-align: left;")
txtstream.WriteLine("    white-Space: nowrap;")
txtstream.WriteLine(" Next")
txtstream.WriteLine("div")
txtstream.WriteLine("")
txtstream.WriteLine("    COLOR: white;")
txtstream.WriteLine("    BACKGROUND-COLOR: black;")
txtstream.WriteLine("    FONT-FAMILY: Cambria, serif;")
txtstream.WriteLine("    FONT-SIZE: 10px;")
txtstream.WriteLine("    text-align: left;")
txtstream.WriteLine("    white-Space: nowrap;")
txtstream.WriteLine(" Next")
txtstream.WriteLine("span")
txtstream.WriteLine("")
txtstream.WriteLine("    COLOR: white;")
txtstream.WriteLine("    BACKGROUND-COLOR: black;")
txtstream.WriteLine("    FONT-FAMILY: Cambria, serif;")
txtstream.WriteLine("    FONT-SIZE: 10px;")
```

```
txtstream.WriteLine("    text-align: left;")
txtstream.WriteLine("    white-Space: nowrap;")
txtstream.WriteLine("    display:inline-block;")
txtstream.WriteLine("    width: 100%;")
txtstream.WriteLine(" Next")
txtstream.WriteLine("textarea")
txtstream.WriteLine("")
txtstream.WriteLine("    COLOR: white;")
txtstream.WriteLine("    BACKGROUND-COLOR: black;")
txtstream.WriteLine("    FONT-FAMILY: Cambria, serif;")
txtstream.WriteLine("    FONT-SIZE: 10px;")
txtstream.WriteLine("    text-align: left;")
txtstream.WriteLine("    white-Space: nowrap;")
txtstream.WriteLine("    width: 100%;")
txtstream.WriteLine(" Next")
txtstream.WriteLine("select")
txtstream.WriteLine("")
txtstream.WriteLine("    COLOR: white;")
txtstream.WriteLine("    BACKGROUND-COLOR: black;")
txtstream.WriteLine("    FONT-FAMILY: Cambria, serif;")
txtstream.WriteLine("    FONT-SIZE: 10px;")
txtstream.WriteLine("    text-align: left;")
txtstream.WriteLine("    white-Space: nowrap;")
txtstream.WriteLine("    width: 100%;")
txtstream.WriteLine(" Next")
txtstream.WriteLine("input")
txtstream.WriteLine("")
txtstream.WriteLine("    COLOR: white;")
txtstream.WriteLine("    BACKGROUND-COLOR: black;")
txtstream.WriteLine("    FONT-FAMILY: Cambria, serif;")
txtstream.WriteLine("    FONT-SIZE: 12px;")
txtstream.WriteLine("    text-align: left;")
txtstream.WriteLine("    display:table-cell;")
txtstream.WriteLine("    white-Space: nowrap;")
txtstream.WriteLine(" Next")
txtstream.WriteLine("h1 ")
txtstream.WriteLine("color: antiquewhite;")
txtstream.WriteLine("text-shadow: 1px 1px 1px black;")
txtstream.WriteLine("padding: 3px;")
txtstream.WriteLine("text-align: center;")
```

txtstream.WriteLine("box-shadow: inSet 2px 2px 5px rgba(0,0,0,0.5), inSet -2px -2px 5px rgba(255,255,255,0.5);")
txtstream.WriteLine(" Next")
txtstream.WriteLine("</style>")
COLORED TEXT

txtstream.WriteLine("<style type='text/css'>")
txtstream.WriteLine("th")
txtstream.WriteLine("")
txtstream.WriteLine("   COLOR: darkred;")
txtstream.WriteLine("   BACKGROUND-COLOR: #eeeeee;")
txtstream.WriteLine("   FONT-FAMILY: Cambria, serif;")
txtstream.WriteLine("   FONT-SIZE: 12px;")
txtstream.WriteLine("   text-align: left;")
txtstream.WriteLine("   white-Space: nowrap;")
txtstream.WriteLine(" Next")
txtstream.WriteLine("td")
txtstream.WriteLine("")
txtstream.WriteLine("   COLOR: navy;")
txtstream.WriteLine("   BACKGROUND-COLOR: #eeeeee;")
txtstream.WriteLine("   FONT-FAMILY: Cambria, serif;")
txtstream.WriteLine("   FONT-SIZE: 12px;")
txtstream.WriteLine("   text-align: left;")
txtstream.WriteLine("   white-Space: nowrap;")
txtstream.WriteLine(" Next")
txtstream.WriteLine("div")
txtstream.WriteLine("")
txtstream.WriteLine("   COLOR: white;")
txtstream.WriteLine("   BACKGROUND-COLOR: navy;")
txtstream.WriteLine("   FONT-FAMILY: Cambria, serif;")
txtstream.WriteLine("   FONT-SIZE: 10px;")
txtstream.WriteLine("   text-align: left;")
txtstream.WriteLine("   white-Space: nowrap;")
txtstream.WriteLine(" Next")
txtstream.WriteLine("span")
txtstream.WriteLine("")
txtstream.WriteLine("   COLOR: white;")
txtstream.WriteLine("   BACKGROUND-COLOR: navy;")
txtstream.WriteLine("   FONT-FAMILY: Cambria, serif;")
txtstream.WriteLine("   FONT-SIZE: 10px;")

```
txtstream.WriteLine("    text-align: left;")
txtstream.WriteLine("    white-Space: nowrap;")
txtstream.WriteLine("    display:inline-block;")
txtstream.WriteLine("    width: 100%;")
txtstream.WriteLine(" Next")
txtstream.WriteLine("textarea")
txtstream.WriteLine("{")
txtstream.WriteLine("    COLOR: white;")
txtstream.WriteLine("    BACKGROUND-COLOR: navy;")
txtstream.WriteLine("    FONT-FAMILY: Cambria, serif;")
txtstream.WriteLine("    FONT-SIZE: 10px;")
txtstream.WriteLine("    text-align: left;")
txtstream.WriteLine("    white-Space: nowrap;")
txtstream.WriteLine("    width: 100%;")
txtstream.WriteLine(" Next")
txtstream.WriteLine("select")
txtstream.WriteLine("{")
txtstream.WriteLine("    COLOR: white;")
txtstream.WriteLine("    BACKGROUND-COLOR: navy;")
txtstream.WriteLine("    FONT-FAMILY: Cambria, serif;")
txtstream.WriteLine("    FONT-SIZE: 10px;")
txtstream.WriteLine("    text-align: left;")
txtstream.WriteLine("    white-Space: nowrap;")
txtstream.WriteLine("    width: 100%;")
txtstream.WriteLine(" Next")
txtstream.WriteLine("input")
txtstream.WriteLine("{")
txtstream.WriteLine("    COLOR: white;")
txtstream.WriteLine("    BACKGROUND-COLOR: navy;")
txtstream.WriteLine("    FONT-FAMILY: Cambria, serif;")
txtstream.WriteLine("    FONT-SIZE: 12px;")
txtstream.WriteLine("    text-align: left;")
txtstream.WriteLine("    display:table-cell;")
txtstream.WriteLine("    white-Space: nowrap;")
txtstream.WriteLine(" Next")
txtstream.WriteLine("h1 ")
txtstream.WriteLine("color: antiquewhite;")
txtstream.WriteLine("text-shadow: 1px 1px 1px black;")
txtstream.WriteLine("padding: 3px;")
txtstream.WriteLine("text-align: center;")
```

txtstream.WriteLine("box-shadow: inSet 2px 2px 5px rgba(0,0,0,0.5), inSet -2px -2px 5px rgba(255,255,255,0.5);")
txtstream.WriteLine(" Next")
txtstream.WriteLine("</style>")

OSCILLATING ROW COLORS

txtstream.WriteLine("<style>")
txtstream.WriteLine("th")
txtstream.WriteLine("")
txtstream.WriteLine("   COLOR: white;")
txtstream.WriteLine("   BACKGROUND-COLOR: navy;")
txtstream.WriteLine("   FONT-FAMILY: Cambria, serif;")
txtstream.WriteLine("   FONT-SIZE: 12px;")
txtstream.WriteLine("   text-align: left;")
txtstream.WriteLine("   white-Space: nowrap;")
txtstream.WriteLine(" Next")
txtstream.WriteLine("td")
txtstream.WriteLine("")
txtstream.WriteLine("   COLOR: navy;")
txtstream.WriteLine("   FONT-FAMILY: Cambria, serif;")
txtstream.WriteLine("   FONT-SIZE: 12px;")
txtstream.WriteLine("   text-align: left;")
txtstream.WriteLine("   white-Space: nowrap;")
txtstream.WriteLine(" Next")
txtstream.WriteLine("div")
txtstream.WriteLine("")
txtstream.WriteLine("   COLOR: navy;")
txtstream.WriteLine("   FONT-FAMILY: Cambria, serif;")
txtstream.WriteLine("   FONT-SIZE: 12px;")
txtstream.WriteLine("   text-align: left;")
txtstream.WriteLine("   white-Space: nowrap;")
txtstream.WriteLine(" Next")
txtstream.WriteLine("span")
txtstream.WriteLine("")
txtstream.WriteLine("   COLOR: navy;")
txtstream.WriteLine("   FONT-FAMILY: Cambria, serif;")
txtstream.WriteLine("   FONT-SIZE: 12px;")

```
txtstream.WriteLine("    text-align: left;")
txtstream.WriteLine("    white-Space: nowrap;")
txtstream.WriteLine("    width: 100%;")
txtstream.WriteLine(" Next")
txtstream.WriteLine("textarea")
txtstream.WriteLine("")
txtstream.WriteLine("    COLOR: navy;")
txtstream.WriteLine("    FONT-FAMILY: Cambria, serif;")
txtstream.WriteLine("    FONT-SIZE: 12px;")
txtstream.WriteLine("    text-align: left;")
txtstream.WriteLine("    white-Space: nowrap;")
txtstream.WriteLine("    display:inline-block;")
txtstream.WriteLine("    width: 100%;")
txtstream.WriteLine(" Next")
txtstream.WriteLine("select")
txtstream.WriteLine("")
txtstream.WriteLine("    COLOR: navy;")
txtstream.WriteLine("    FONT-FAMILY: Cambria, serif;")
txtstream.WriteLine("    FONT-SIZE: 10px;")
txtstream.WriteLine("    text-align: left;")
txtstream.WriteLine("    white-Space: nowrap;")
txtstream.WriteLine("    display:inline-block;")
txtstream.WriteLine("    width: 100%;")
txtstream.WriteLine(" Next")
txtstream.WriteLine("input")
txtstream.WriteLine("")
txtstream.WriteLine("    COLOR: navy;")
txtstream.WriteLine("    FONT-FAMILY: Cambria, serif;")
txtstream.WriteLine("    FONT-SIZE: 12px;")
txtstream.WriteLine("    text-align: left;")
txtstream.WriteLine("    display:table-cell;")
txtstream.WriteLine("    white-Space: nowrap;")
txtstream.WriteLine(" Next")
txtstream.WriteLine("h1 ")
txtstream.WriteLine("color: antiquewhite;")
txtstream.WriteLine("text-shadow: 1px 1px 1px black;")
txtstream.WriteLine("padding: 3px;")
txtstream.WriteLine("text-align: center;")
txtstream.WriteLine("box-shadow: inSet 2px 2px 5px rgba(0,0,0,0.5), inSet -2px
-2px 5px rgba(255,255,255,0.5);")
```

txtstream.WriteLine(" Next")
txtstream.WriteLine("tr:nth-child(even)background-color:#f2f2f2; Next")
txtstream.WriteLine("tr:nth-child(odd)background-color:#cccccc; color:#f2f2f2; Next")
txtstream.WriteLine("</style>")

GHOST DECORATED

txtstream.WriteLine("<style type='text/css'>")
txtstream.WriteLine("th")
txtstream.WriteLine("")
txtstream.WriteLine("   COLOR: black;")
txtstream.WriteLine("   BACKGROUND-COLOR: white;")
txtstream.WriteLine("   FONT-FAMILY: Cambria, serif;")
txtstream.WriteLine("   FONT-SIZE: 12px;")
txtstream.WriteLine("   text-align: left;")
txtstream.WriteLine("   white-Space: nowrap;")
txtstream.WriteLine(" Next")
txtstream.WriteLine("td")
txtstream.WriteLine("")
txtstream.WriteLine("   COLOR: black;")
txtstream.WriteLine("   BACKGROUND-COLOR: white;")
txtstream.WriteLine("   FONT-FAMILY: Cambria, serif;")
txtstream.WriteLine("   FONT-SIZE: 12px;")
txtstream.WriteLine("   text-align: left;")
txtstream.WriteLine("   white-Space: nowrap;")
txtstream.WriteLine(" Next")
txtstream.WriteLine("div")
txtstream.WriteLine("")
txtstream.WriteLine("   COLOR: black;")
txtstream.WriteLine("   BACKGROUND-COLOR: white;")
txtstream.WriteLine("   FONT-FAMILY: Cambria, serif;")
txtstream.WriteLine("   FONT-SIZE: 10px;")
txtstream.WriteLine("   text-align: left;")
txtstream.WriteLine("   white-Space: nowrap;")
txtstream.WriteLine(" Next")
txtstream.WriteLine("span")
txtstream.WriteLine("")
txtstream.WriteLine("   COLOR: black;")
txtstream.WriteLine("   BACKGROUND-COLOR: white;")

```
txtstream.WriteLine("    FONT-FAMILY: Cambria, serif;")
txtstream.WriteLine("    FONT-SIZE: 10px;")
txtstream.WriteLine("    text-align: left;")
txtstream.WriteLine("    white-Space: nowrap;")
txtstream.WriteLine("    display:inline-block;")
txtstream.WriteLine("    width: 100%;")
txtstream.WriteLine(" Next")
txtstream.WriteLine("textarea")
txtstream.WriteLine("")
txtstream.WriteLine("    COLOR: black;")
txtstream.WriteLine("    BACKGROUND-COLOR: white;")
txtstream.WriteLine("    FONT-FAMILY: Cambria, serif;")
txtstream.WriteLine("    FONT-SIZE: 10px;")
txtstream.WriteLine("    text-align: left;")
txtstream.WriteLine("    white-Space: nowrap;")
txtstream.WriteLine("    width: 100%;")
txtstream.WriteLine(" Next")
txtstream.WriteLine("select")
txtstream.WriteLine("")
txtstream.WriteLine("    COLOR: black;")
txtstream.WriteLine("    BACKGROUND-COLOR: white;")
txtstream.WriteLine("    FONT-FAMILY: Cambria, serif;")
txtstream.WriteLine("    FONT-SIZE: 10px;")
txtstream.WriteLine("    text-align: left;")
txtstream.WriteLine("    white-Space: nowrap;")
txtstream.WriteLine("    width: 100%;")
txtstream.WriteLine(" Next")
txtstream.WriteLine("input")
txtstream.WriteLine("")
txtstream.WriteLine("    COLOR: black;")
txtstream.WriteLine("    BACKGROUND-COLOR: white;")
txtstream.WriteLine("    FONT-FAMILY: Cambria, serif;")
txtstream.WriteLine("    FONT-SIZE: 12px;")
txtstream.WriteLine("    text-align: left;")
txtstream.WriteLine("    display:table-cell;")
txtstream.WriteLine("    white-Space: nowrap;")
txtstream.WriteLine(" Next")
txtstream.WriteLine("h1 ")
txtstream.WriteLine("color: antiquewhite;")
txtstream.WriteLine("text-shadow: 1px 1px 1px black;")
```

txtstream.WriteLine("padding: 3px;")
txtstream.WriteLine("text-align: center;")
txtstream.WriteLine("box-shadow: inSet 2px 2px 5px rgba(0,0,0,0.5), inSet -2px -2px 5px rgba(255,255,255,0.5);")
txtstream.WriteLine(" Next")
txtstream.WriteLine("</style>")

3D

txtstream.WriteLine("<style type='text/css'>")
txtstream.WriteLine("body")
txtstream.WriteLine("")
txtstream.WriteLine("   PADDING-RIGHT: 0px;")
txtstream.WriteLine("   PADDING-LEFT: 0px;")
txtstream.WriteLine("   PADDING-BOTTOM: 0px;")
txtstream.WriteLine("   MARGIN: 0px;")
txtstream.WriteLine("   COLOR: #333;")
txtstream.WriteLine("   PADDING-TOP: 0px;")
txtstream.WriteLine("   FONT-FAMILY: verdana, arial, helvetica, sans-serif;")
txtstream.WriteLine(" Next")
txtstream.WriteLine("table")
txtstream.WriteLine("")
txtstream.WriteLine("   BORDER-RIGHT: #999999 3px solid;")
txtstream.WriteLine("   PADDING-RIGHT: 6px;")
txtstream.WriteLine("   PADDING-LEFT: 6px;")
txtstream.WriteLine("   FONT-WEIGHT: Bold;")
txtstream.WriteLine("   FONT-SIZE: 14px;")
txtstream.WriteLine("   PADDING-BOTTOM: 6px;")
txtstream.WriteLine("   COLOR: Peru;")
txtstream.WriteLine("   LINE-HEIGHT: 14px;")
txtstream.WriteLine("   PADDING-TOP: 6px;")
txtstream.WriteLine("   BORDER-BOTTOM: #999 1px solid;")
txtstream.WriteLine("   BACKGROUND-COLOR: #eeeeee;")
txtstream.WriteLine("   FONT-FAMILY: verdana, arial, helvetica, sans-serif;")
txtstream.WriteLine("   FONT-SIZE: 12px;")
txtstream.WriteLine(" Next")
txtstream.WriteLine("th")
txtstream.WriteLine("")
txtstream.WriteLine("   BORDER-RIGHT: #999999 3px solid;")

```
txtstream.WriteLine("    PADDING-RIGHT: 6px;")
txtstream.WriteLine("    PADDING-LEFT: 6px;")
txtstream.WriteLine("    FONT-WEIGHT: Bold;")
txtstream.WriteLine("    FONT-SIZE: 14px;")
txtstream.WriteLine("    PADDING-BOTTOM: 6px;")
txtstream.WriteLine("    COLOR: darkred;")
txtstream.WriteLine("    LINE-HEIGHT: 14px;")
txtstream.WriteLine("    PADDING-TOP: 6px;")
txtstream.WriteLine("    BORDER-BOTTOM: #999 1px solid;")
txtstream.WriteLine("    BACKGROUND-COLOR: #eeeeee;")
txtstream.WriteLine("    FONT-FAMILY: Cambria, serif;")
txtstream.WriteLine("    FONT-SIZE: 12px;")
txtstream.WriteLine("    text-align: left;")
txtstream.WriteLine("    white-Space: nowrap;")
txtstream.WriteLine(" Next")
txtstream.WriteLine(".th")
txtstream.WriteLine("")
txtstream.WriteLine("    BORDER-RIGHT: #999999 2px solid;")
txtstream.WriteLine("    PADDING-RIGHT: 6px;")
txtstream.WriteLine("    PADDING-LEFT: 6px;")
txtstream.WriteLine("    FONT-WEIGHT: Bold;")
txtstream.WriteLine("    PADDING-BOTTOM: 6px;")
txtstream.WriteLine("    COLOR: black;")
txtstream.WriteLine("    PADDING-TOP: 6px;")
txtstream.WriteLine("    BORDER-BOTTOM: #999 2px solid;")
txtstream.WriteLine("    BACKGROUND-COLOR: #eeeeee;")
txtstream.WriteLine("    FONT-FAMILY: Cambria, serif;")
txtstream.WriteLine("    FONT-SIZE: 10px;")
txtstream.WriteLine("    text-align: right;")
txtstream.WriteLine("    white-Space: nowrap;")
txtstream.WriteLine(" Next")
txtstream.WriteLine("td")
txtstream.WriteLine("")
txtstream.WriteLine("    BORDER-RIGHT: #999999 3px solid;")
txtstream.WriteLine("    PADDING-RIGHT: 6px;")
txtstream.WriteLine("    PADDING-LEFT: 6px;")
txtstream.WriteLine("    FONT-WEIGHT: Normal;")
txtstream.WriteLine("    PADDING-BOTTOM: 6px;")
txtstream.WriteLine("    COLOR: navy;")
txtstream.WriteLine("    LINE-HEIGHT: 14px;")
```

```
txtstream.WriteLine("    PADDING-TOP: 6px;")
txtstream.WriteLine("    BORDER-BOTTOM: #999 1px solid;")
txtstream.WriteLine("    BACKGROUND-COLOR: #eeeeee;")
txtstream.WriteLine("    FONT-FAMILY: Cambria, serif;")
txtstream.WriteLine("    FONT-SIZE: 12px;")
txtstream.WriteLine("    text-align: left;")
txtstream.WriteLine("    white-Space: nowrap;")
txtstream.WriteLine(" Next")
txtstream.WriteLine("div")
txtstream.WriteLine("")
txtstream.WriteLine("    BORDER-RIGHT: #999999 3px solid;")
txtstream.WriteLine("    PADDING-RIGHT: 6px;")
txtstream.WriteLine("    PADDING-LEFT: 6px;")
txtstream.WriteLine("    FONT-WEIGHT: Normal;")
txtstream.WriteLine("    PADDING-BOTTOM: 6px;")
txtstream.WriteLine("    COLOR: white;")
txtstream.WriteLine("    PADDING-TOP: 6px;")
txtstream.WriteLine("    BORDER-BOTTOM: #999 1px solid;")
txtstream.WriteLine("    BACKGROUND-COLOR: navy;")
txtstream.WriteLine("    FONT-FAMILY: Cambria, serif;")
txtstream.WriteLine("    FONT-SIZE: 10px;")
txtstream.WriteLine("    text-align: left;")
txtstream.WriteLine("    white-Space: nowrap;")
txtstream.WriteLine(" Next")
txtstream.WriteLine("span")
txtstream.WriteLine("")
txtstream.WriteLine("    BORDER-RIGHT: #999999 3px solid;")
txtstream.WriteLine("    PADDING-RIGHT: 3px;")
txtstream.WriteLine("    PADDING-LEFT: 3px;")
txtstream.WriteLine("    FONT-WEIGHT: Normal;")
txtstream.WriteLine("    PADDING-BOTTOM: 3px;")
txtstream.WriteLine("    COLOR: white;")
txtstream.WriteLine("    PADDING-TOP: 3px;")
txtstream.WriteLine("    BORDER-BOTTOM: #999 1px solid;")
txtstream.WriteLine("    BACKGROUND-COLOR: navy;")
txtstream.WriteLine("    FONT-FAMILY: Cambria, serif;")
txtstream.WriteLine("    FONT-SIZE: 10px;")
txtstream.WriteLine("    text-align: left;")
txtstream.WriteLine("    white-Space: nowrap;")
txtstream.WriteLine("    display:inline-block;")
```

```
txtstream.WriteLine("    width: 100%;")
txtstream.WriteLine(" Next")
txtstream.WriteLine("textarea")
txtstream.WriteLine("")
txtstream.WriteLine("    BORDER-RIGHT: #999999 3px solid;")
txtstream.WriteLine("    PADDING-RIGHT: 3px;")
txtstream.WriteLine("    PADDING-LEFT: 3px;")
txtstream.WriteLine("    FONT-WEIGHT: Normal;")
txtstream.WriteLine("    PADDING-BOTTOM: 3px;")
txtstream.WriteLine("    COLOR: white;")
txtstream.WriteLine("    PADDING-TOP: 3px;")
txtstream.WriteLine("    BORDER-BOTTOM: #999 1px solid;")
txtstream.WriteLine("    BACKGROUND-COLOR: navy;")
txtstream.WriteLine("    FONT-FAMILY: Cambria, serif;")
txtstream.WriteLine("    FONT-SIZE: 10px;")
txtstream.WriteLine("    text-align: left;")
txtstream.WriteLine("    white-Space: nowrap;")
txtstream.WriteLine("    width: 100%;")
txtstream.WriteLine(" Next")
txtstream.WriteLine("select")
txtstream.WriteLine("")
txtstream.WriteLine("    BORDER-RIGHT: #999999 3px solid;")
txtstream.WriteLine("    PADDING-RIGHT: 6px;")
txtstream.WriteLine("    PADDING-LEFT: 6px;")
txtstream.WriteLine("    FONT-WEIGHT: Normal;")
txtstream.WriteLine("    PADDING-BOTTOM: 6px;")
txtstream.WriteLine("    COLOR: white;")
txtstream.WriteLine("    PADDING-TOP: 6px;")
txtstream.WriteLine("    BORDER-BOTTOM: #999 1px solid;")
txtstream.WriteLine("    BACKGROUND-COLOR: navy;")
txtstream.WriteLine("    FONT-FAMILY: Cambria, serif;")
txtstream.WriteLine("    FONT-SIZE: 10px;")
txtstream.WriteLine("    text-align: left;")
txtstream.WriteLine("    white-Space: nowrap;")
txtstream.WriteLine("    width: 100%;")
txtstream.WriteLine(" Next")
txtstream.WriteLine("input")
txtstream.WriteLine("")
txtstream.WriteLine("    BORDER-RIGHT: #999999 3px solid;")
txtstream.WriteLine("    PADDING-RIGHT: 3px;")
```

```
txtstream.WriteLine("    PADDING-LEFT: 3px;")
txtstream.WriteLine("    FONT-WEIGHT: Bold;")
txtstream.WriteLine("    PADDING-BOTTOM: 3px;")
txtstream.WriteLine("    COLOR: white;")
txtstream.WriteLine("    PADDING-TOP: 3px;")
txtstream.WriteLine("    BORDER-BOTTOM: #999 1px solid;")
txtstream.WriteLine("    BACKGROUND-COLOR: navy;")
txtstream.WriteLine("    FONT-FAMILY: Cambria, serif;")
txtstream.WriteLine("    FONT-SIZE: 12px;")
txtstream.WriteLine("    text-align: left;")
txtstream.WriteLine("    display:table-cell;")
txtstream.WriteLine("    white-Space: nowrap;")
txtstream.WriteLine("    width: 100%;")
txtstream.WriteLine(" Next")
txtstream.WriteLine("h1 ")
txtstream.WriteLine("color: antiquewhite;")
txtstream.WriteLine("text-shadow: 1px 1px 1px black;")
txtstream.WriteLine("padding: 3px;")
txtstream.WriteLine("text-align: center;")
txtstream.WriteLine("box-shadow: inSet 2px 2px 5px rgba(0,0,0,0.5), inSet -2px
-2px 5px rgba(255,255,255,0.5);")
txtstream.WriteLine(" Next")
txtstream.WriteLine("</style>")
```

SHADOW BOX

```
txtstream.WriteLine("<style type='text/css'>")
txtstream.WriteLine("body")
txtstream.WriteLine("")
txtstream.WriteLine("    PADDING-RIGHT: 0px;")
txtstream.WriteLine("    PADDING-LEFT: 0px;")
txtstream.WriteLine("    PADDING-BOTTOM: 0px;")
txtstream.WriteLine("    MARGIN: 0px;")
txtstream.WriteLine("    COLOR: #333;")
txtstream.WriteLine("    PADDING-TOP: 0px;")
txtstream.WriteLine("    FONT-FAMILY:  verdana, arial, helvetica, sans-serif;")
txtstream.WriteLine(" Next")
txtstream.WriteLine("table")
txtstream.WriteLine("")
txtstream.WriteLine("    BORDER-RIGHT: #999999 1px solid;")
```

```
txtstream.WriteLine("    PADDING-RIGHT: 1px;")
txtstream.WriteLine("    PADDING-LEFT: 1px;")
txtstream.WriteLine("    PADDING-BOTTOM: 1px;")
txtstream.WriteLine("    LINE-HEIGHT: 8px;")
txtstream.WriteLine("    PADDING-TOP: 1px;")
txtstream.WriteLine("    BORDER-BOTTOM: #999 1px solid;")
txtstream.WriteLine("    BACKGROUND-COLOR: #eeeeee;")
txtstream.WriteLine("
filter:progid:DXImageTransform.Microsoft.Shadow(color='silver',    Direction=135,
Strength=16)")
txtstream.WriteLine(" Next")
txtstream.WriteLine("th")
txtstream.WriteLine("")
txtstream.WriteLine("    BORDER-RIGHT: #999999 3px solid;")
txtstream.WriteLine("    PADDING-RIGHT: 6px;")
txtstream.WriteLine("    PADDING-LEFT: 6px;")
txtstream.WriteLine("    FONT-WEIGHT: Bold;")
txtstream.WriteLine("    FONT-SIZE: 14px;")
txtstream.WriteLine("    PADDING-BOTTOM: 6px;")
txtstream.WriteLine("    COLOR: darkred;")
txtstream.WriteLine("    LINE-HEIGHT: 14px;")
txtstream.WriteLine("    PADDING-TOP: 6px;")
txtstream.WriteLine("    BORDER-BOTTOM: #999 1px solid;")
txtstream.WriteLine("    BACKGROUND-COLOR: #eeeeee;")
txtstream.WriteLine("    FONT-FAMILY: Cambria, serif;")
txtstream.WriteLine("    FONT-SIZE: 12px;")
txtstream.WriteLine("    text-align: left;")
txtstream.WriteLine("    white-Space: nowrap;")
txtstream.WriteLine(" Next")
txtstream.WriteLine(".th")
txtstream.WriteLine("")
txtstream.WriteLine("    BORDER-RIGHT: #999999 2px solid;")
txtstream.WriteLine("    PADDING-RIGHT: 6px;")
txtstream.WriteLine("    PADDING-LEFT: 6px;")
txtstream.WriteLine("    FONT-WEIGHT: Bold;")
txtstream.WriteLine("    PADDING-BOTTOM: 6px;")
txtstream.WriteLine("    COLOR: black;")
txtstream.WriteLine("    PADDING-TOP: 6px;")
txtstream.WriteLine("    BORDER-BOTTOM: #999 2px solid;")
txtstream.WriteLine("    BACKGROUND-COLOR: #eeeeee;")
```

```
txtstream.WriteLine("    FONT-FAMILY: Cambria, serif;")
txtstream.WriteLine("    FONT-SIZE: 10px;")
txtstream.WriteLine("    text-align: right;")
txtstream.WriteLine("    white-Space: nowrap;")
txtstream.WriteLine(" Next")
txtstream.WriteLine("td")
txtstream.WriteLine("")
txtstream.WriteLine("    BORDER-RIGHT: #999999 3px solid;")
txtstream.WriteLine("    PADDING-RIGHT: 6px;")
txtstream.WriteLine("    PADDING-LEFT: 6px;")
txtstream.WriteLine("    FONT-WEIGHT: Normal;")
txtstream.WriteLine("    PADDING-BOTTOM: 6px;")
txtstream.WriteLine("    COLOR: navy;")
txtstream.WriteLine("    LINE-HEIGHT: 14px;")
txtstream.WriteLine("    PADDING-TOP: 6px;")
txtstream.WriteLine("    BORDER-BOTTOM: #999 1px solid;")
txtstream.WriteLine("    BACKGROUND-COLOR: #eeeeee;")
txtstream.WriteLine("    FONT-FAMILY: Cambria, serif;")
txtstream.WriteLine("    FONT-SIZE: 12px;")
txtstream.WriteLine("    text-align: left;")
txtstream.WriteLine("    white-Space: nowrap;")
txtstream.WriteLine(" Next")
txtstream.WriteLine("div")
txtstream.WriteLine("")
txtstream.WriteLine("    BORDER-RIGHT: #999999 3px solid;")
txtstream.WriteLine("    PADDING-RIGHT: 6px;")
txtstream.WriteLine("    PADDING-LEFT: 6px;")
txtstream.WriteLine("    FONT-WEIGHT: Normal;")
txtstream.WriteLine("    PADDING-BOTTOM: 6px;")
txtstream.WriteLine("    COLOR: white;")
txtstream.WriteLine("    PADDING-TOP: 6px;")
txtstream.WriteLine("    BORDER-BOTTOM: #999 1px solid;")
txtstream.WriteLine("    BACKGROUND-COLOR: navy;")
txtstream.WriteLine("    FONT-FAMILY: Cambria, serif;")
txtstream.WriteLine("    FONT-SIZE: 10px;")
txtstream.WriteLine("    text-align: left;")
txtstream.WriteLine("    white-Space: nowrap;")
txtstream.WriteLine(" Next")
txtstream.WriteLine("span")
txtstream.WriteLine("")
```

```
txtstream.WriteLine("    BORDER-RIGHT: #999999 3px solid;")
txtstream.WriteLine("    PADDING-RIGHT: 3px;")
txtstream.WriteLine("    PADDING-LEFT: 3px;")
txtstream.WriteLine("    FONT-WEIGHT: Normal;")
txtstream.WriteLine("    PADDING-BOTTOM: 3px;")
txtstream.WriteLine("    COLOR: white;")
txtstream.WriteLine("    PADDING-TOP: 3px;")
txtstream.WriteLine("    BORDER-BOTTOM: #999 1px solid;")
txtstream.WriteLine("    BACKGROUND-COLOR: navy;")
txtstream.WriteLine("    FONT-FAMILY: Cambria, serif;")
txtstream.WriteLine("    FONT-SIZE: 10px;")
txtstream.WriteLine("    text-align: left;")
txtstream.WriteLine("    white-Space: nowrap;")
txtstream.WriteLine("    display: inline-block;")
txtstream.WriteLine("    width: 100%;")
txtstream.WriteLine(" Next")
txtstream.WriteLine("textarea")
txtstream.WriteLine("")
txtstream.WriteLine("    BORDER-RIGHT: #999999 3px solid;")
txtstream.WriteLine("    PADDING-RIGHT: 3px;")
txtstream.WriteLine("    PADDING-LEFT: 3px;")
txtstream.WriteLine("    FONT-WEIGHT: Normal;")
txtstream.WriteLine("    PADDING-BOTTOM: 3px;")
txtstream.WriteLine("    COLOR: white;")
txtstream.WriteLine("    PADDING-TOP: 3px;")
txtstream.WriteLine("    BORDER-BOTTOM: #999 1px solid;")
txtstream.WriteLine("    BACKGROUND-COLOR: navy;")
txtstream.WriteLine("    FONT-FAMILY: Cambria, serif;")
txtstream.WriteLine("    FONT-SIZE: 10px;")
txtstream.WriteLine("    text-align: left;")
txtstream.WriteLine("    white-Space: nowrap;")
txtstream.WriteLine("    width: 100%;")
txtstream.WriteLine(" Next")
txtstream.WriteLine("select")
txtstream.WriteLine("")
txtstream.WriteLine("    BORDER-RIGHT: #999999 3px solid;")
txtstream.WriteLine("    PADDING-RIGHT: 6px;")
txtstream.WriteLine("    PADDING-LEFT: 6px;")
txtstream.WriteLine("    FONT-WEIGHT: Normal;")
txtstream.WriteLine("    PADDING-BOTTOM: 6px;")
```

```
txtstream.WriteLine("   COLOR: white;")
txtstream.WriteLine("   PADDING-TOP: 6px;")
txtstream.WriteLine("   BORDER-BOTTOM: #999 1px solid;")
txtstream.WriteLine("   BACKGROUND-COLOR: navy;")
txtstream.WriteLine("   FONT-FAMILY: Cambria, serif;")
txtstream.WriteLine("   FONT-SIZE: 10px;")
txtstream.WriteLine("   text-align: left;")
txtstream.WriteLine("   white-Space: nowrap;")
txtstream.WriteLine("   width: 100%;")
txtstream.WriteLine(" Next")
txtstream.WriteLine("input")
txtstream.WriteLine("")
txtstream.WriteLine("   BORDER-RIGHT: #999999 3px solid;")
txtstream.WriteLine("   PADDING-RIGHT: 3px;")
txtstream.WriteLine("   PADDING-LEFT: 3px;")
txtstream.WriteLine("   FONT-WEIGHT: Bold;")
txtstream.WriteLine("   PADDING-BOTTOM: 3px;")
txtstream.WriteLine("   COLOR: white;")
txtstream.WriteLine("   PADDING-TOP: 3px;")
txtstream.WriteLine("   BORDER-BOTTOM: #999 1px solid;")
txtstream.WriteLine("   BACKGROUND-COLOR: navy;")
txtstream.WriteLine("   FONT-FAMILY: Cambria, serif;")
txtstream.WriteLine("   FONT-SIZE: 12px;")
txtstream.WriteLine("   text-align: left;")
txtstream.WriteLine("   display: table-cell;")
txtstream.WriteLine("   white-Space: nowrap;")
txtstream.WriteLine("   width: 100%;")
txtstream.WriteLine(" Next")
txtstream.WriteLine("h1 ")
txtstream.WriteLine("color: antiquewhite;")
txtstream.WriteLine("text-shadow: 1px 1px 1px black;")
txtstream.WriteLine("padding: 3px;")
txtstream.WriteLine("text-align: center;")
txtstream.WriteLine("box-shadow: inSet 2px 2px 5px rgba(0,0,0,0.5), inSet -2px -2px 5px rgba(255,255,255,0.5);")
txtstream.WriteLine(" Next")
txtstream.WriteLine("</style>")
```